"Willow does not hold back! If you want the real deal, the raw, vulnerable story of one woman's life journey from extreme struggle to peace and happiness, Willow delivers."
—Aleta Norris, Bestselling author
of Women Who Spark.

"Willow shares her journey, her pain and her transformation honestly and insightfully, inviting you to make changes in your own life. The book is full of practical steps to take and questions to ask!"
—John Antonio, Author of Always Say Hi

"One of the first necessary steps to self-transformation is recognizing the places within you that are stuck cycling through old worn out belief patterns. Willow does a beautiful job of illuminating these spaces through sharing her personal experiences in a way that allows her readers to relate and identify these patterns within themselves. She then offers poignant reflective exercises and questions to usher in new ways of being. Written with love, and a deep sense of respect, this book is a must read for all spiritual seekers looking to shift their mindsets towards self-love, happiness, and success."
—Gabrielle Sisson, LMT, Herbalist, Nutritional
Consultant, Birth Coach, Energy Worker

"Powerful, vulnerable and written in a way to unlock new possibilities. Willow shares her journey, her pain and her transformation in a way that invites you to make changes in your own life. Not only could I see myself, but Willow also gives the necessary steps to turn traumatic experiences into triumphant lessons. The questions she asks really allowed me to shift my perception."
—Lori Schmeichel Jones

"I had the honor of reading an advanced copy of Willow Green's transformational autobiography, Rewriting Your Reality.

Green's second book is profound. The author's ability to peel back the layers of the human experience, exposing the raw and vulnerable evolution we all endure, is refreshingly real.

Her willingness to explore the dark sides of her psyche, alongside the startlingly honest, and even selfish perspectives we can so easily indulge, allows the reader to openly reflect on their own learnings and stories.

Green creates the space, but importantly, compels the reader to dig deeper, and push beyond assumptions or indoctrinated interpretations to pure, unadulterated ego.

When we conclude her story, the humorous, heart breaking, and honest account of her life, we are invited to transform. Rewriting our past, we create our reality. Stepping into and embracing the present moment gives us the permission we all so desperately need to design our desired future.

Thank you Willow Green. You inspire us all."

—Nicole BZ, Business
Expert and Success Strategist, NicoleBZ.com

REWRITING YOUR REALITY

You Have A Choice

A Path to Enlightenment

WILLOW GREEN

Cover Picture by Johnny Wechs

Published by Author Academy Elite

Published in the United States

First Printing 2020

ISBN Paperback: 978-1-64746-043-3
ISBN Hardback: 978-1-64746-044-0
ISBN Ebook: 978-1-64746-045-7

Other books by Willow Green

I'm Sober, Now What? Moving through the fear,
anxiety and humility of LIFE on Life's terms.

Dedication

To You, for taking responsibility for yourself, choosing
a path and living your best life ever!

CONTENTS

FOREWORD

There is no gold in the pot at the end of the rainbow, the pot is empty. The gold is found in nuggets scattered on the path that lead to the pot. The pot is only there as a lure get you off your ass and moving! Because it's only while moving forward on your path that you find the gold nuggets in life that serve to enhance your life...

Golden nuggets are insights, connections, wisdom, resources, love, support, strength, etc.

Everything in your life can become a resource that supports you, an ally. Or, an enemy put on your path to stop you, to destroy your dreams.

What things become is solely based on what you're looking for because everything can be both an ally and an enemy.

One of the greatest and most valuable assets you can find in your journey of life is human vulnerability.

When a person finds the courage to share their story, their challenges, the adversity they experienced in a vulnerable way coupled with authenticity (or not doing it for accolades or to impress others), you will no doubt find an abundance of gold nuggets that can help you gain hope, clarity, focus, and courage in facing your own challenges and adversity in life.

And that's exactly what the author, Willow, has done with this body of work.

Decide what you want to find. And seek that as you read the pages of this book and you will find them in abundance.

Do not dismiss any nugget you find, from a flake to a boulder. Many people dismiss the things they deem as "small". The small insights. The tiny shifts in perspectives. The small expansion of awareness or clarity.

Forgetting that big things are nothing more than a bunch of small things stuck together.

You'll find whatever you look for. Look for what you want to find in this book and it can become a great asset in your life.

And always remember… Highest Energy Wins!

Mike Kemski is a 2-time #1 Bestselling Author and creator of the PowerLife Principles. His focus is not on creating miracles for others, but helping others discover that they have the power to create their own miracles in life. You can find out more about Mike, his books and PowerLife Principles at PowerLifeSystems.com

ACKNOWLEDGEMENTS

Thank you to my mom for the time and space to write this. Thank you for the willingness to take this journey with me, grow with me and become my friend. Thank you for choosing to see.

Thank you Jesse Elder, Mike Kemski and all the Legends, Lighthouses and Freedom Teachers

Thank you Abraham, Esther and Jerry Hicks, Santo Daime, my guides, my wiser self, spiritual family and God, who is within me.

Tupper Lake Community, Jim Frenette and his family and the entire network I met there.

Schenectady Clubhouse and community.

Thank you to all the people who showed me love, kindness and acceptance.

Thank you to those who did not as well.

Special thanks to those not already mentioned who really made a special impact on me:

Spencer Stewart
Stephanie Ansin

Padhrinho Paulo
Lori Schmeichel Jones

Nicole BZ

Cher Gardiner

Lis Rolfe

Marjorie Fratt

Carolina Zarcaria

Greg Nosworthy

Destiny Rochelle Dempsey

Dharma and Jamini

Minh Nguyen

Anne Marie Miller

John Gibson

John Minks

Lance Champagne

Kimberly Fonetenot

Margaret Elaine Moroney

Gabrielle Sisson

Ana Luisa Doria Meunier

Jenifer Rearden

Di Parente

Missy Balsam

Dave Ayote

Myron Lauzon

Gary Testa

Johnny Wechs

Jason Wechs

Jeff McDougall

Amy Larsen

Mike Mcguinnis

John Nebus

Susun Weed

Susan Hughes

INTRODUCTION

Enlightenment has been one of the biggest and most misunderstood journeys, often referred to as a destination rather
than a state of being. The path to enlightenment has led many
to travel the world to find the answers; seeking the Truth, the
Blessings, the gift of enlightenment from those deemed the
chosen ones.

I was one of those seekers, looking, asking, chasing this
thing called enlightenment.

I found it and it was nothing like I thought. It's actually
scary how easy it was when I was ready to see. I had to be ready.
I had to be willing. And I had to surrender.

It is not something to be taught, sought, or delivered. It is
only found within. It truly is a state of Being. Everyone has
access to it. The confusion sets in when we see others, the
select few that are "enlightened", and they are so at peace. It's
that peace, clarity, confidence and inner knowing that we truly
desire. And anyone can have all of that peace, connection, and
all knowing. However very few are willing to take the journey.
It's not an easy journey. It's painful. There is no shortcut, magic

pill, magic medicine or easy path. There is one path, through the illusion.

How do you walk through the illusion? Through self-discovery. Choosing to see yourself, all of yourself, and accepting who you are is the only path to True Enlightenment. It's the process of letting go of everything you thought you knew. You must let go of old stories, old beliefs, attachments to your way of thinking, and everything you thought you knew and be open to seeing a new perspective.

True enlightenment is shedding the layers of attachments. Attachments to things, stories, viewpoints, belief systems. It's the journey of unbecoming and unknowing everything you believed was Truth and really discovering who and what you want now.

It's a choice. A choice to see yourself at the core. If you choose to see, what you will find is Freedom. A freedom beyond what you thought possible, not just time, space, and economic freedom, but beyond that.

You will discover love, connection and inner peace beyond what your mind can comprehend in this moment. As you peel back the layers, you will experience more joy, love, freedom of self-expression.

You will learn to enjoy the contrast, seeing every challenge as another opportunity to go deeper and experience another level of lightness. Each pain, fear, or paralyzing feeling is the door. The door to the next level of enlightenment.

When we open the door, it's terrifying, painful and hurts. However if we are willing to look, to face what we are feeling, seeing and discovering, the process will set you free. Facing our greatest fears is the path to enlightenment.

This doesn't mean run into a burning building, jump out of a plane without a parachute or put yourself in danger. The fears I am referring to are internal, they are the stories, beliefs and perspectives that we hold onto so dearly. They are what we have created that once kept us safe, made us feel good, and protected us.

What protected us as a child, or when we experienced trauma, or were in a fight or flight mode becomes a trap. What once served to protect, connect and help us is the very thing blocking you from having what you desire the most.

The process of looking at why we do what we do and who we are can be scary. I hated myself and who I had become at times. However, once I chose to face myself, my demons, my parts I deemed unlovable, something shifted. I became loveable. I was lighter. I was able to not only love, accept and see myself differently, but also see my brothers, sisters and the world differently.

I discovered a new sense of freedom. I felt love deeper than I knew possible. I experienced understanding, kindness and connection in ways that used to scare me. My health improved. My thoughts were clearer. My heart was lighter. I am experiencing freedom on a level above and beyond what I believed possible. And you can too.

I invite you to be bold, be fearless, and to be brutally honest with yourself. I share vulnerably, honestly, and deeply. I do this in hopes that you can see yourself in me. I ask many questions I asked myself. I share what I went through to show you it's painful, it can be ugly and embarrassing. I made mistakes, I took risks, I had to accept that I was wrong. It was embarrassing. It hurt my ego. And I would do it all over in a heartbeat. Why? Because it freed me.

So again, I invite you to be honest. How you choose to use this book is entirely up to you. However, if you choose to see, to really see yourself, I promise that you will feel lighter. You will have discovered your own path to enlightenment.

True enlightenment is only found within.

SEEKING

(July/ Reflecting over the previous 14 months)

Sitting here, confidence shaken. Have you wanted something so badly that nothing will stop you? You believe it is possible. You feel it in every cell of your body. You breathe it. You fantasize about it. You are so sure that what you desire and think is real that nothing and no one can change your mind. You refuse to listen to what anyone else says. You put yourself out there, really giving it your all, 100% vulnerable, believing without a doubt, everything is going to work out. You have no doubts that this is it!

I have finally found love, purpose, and my dreams are becoming my reality! All my affirmations are finally coming true! Thank you, Universe!

Only to get to the other side and realize while you were so focused on your desire, you completely missed all the red flags. Getting so caught up in the moment, in the dream, that you never once considered how you will be received. All your actions came from the limited perspective of self and motivated by "what I want". And now there you are, alone in the darkness, everything on the line. The dream you created in your mind, only made sense in your mind. No one else seemed to understand or be able to see or hear what you were so sure of. It only made sense to you, and now even you are questioning yourself.

Feeling lost, confused, a little hopeless. Wondering if it's time to throw in the towel on love, purpose and chasing your dreams? Looking over the past and seeing, really seeing all the mistakes you made. Looking at all the ways you could have or should have done it better.

Do you find yourself reflecting on the relationships you chose, the people you allowed into your life and the advice you knew better than taking, but took it anyway? Asking yourself, WHY? Why didn't I trust my gut? I knew better. I knew this wouldn't work out well.

This was me, a version of me, right before I alchemized all those "should haves" and "could haves" and transformed them into little nuggets of wisdom! See, unfortunately we learn through what many call mistakes; I personally like to call them choices. There are no mistakes, only opportunities to gain clarity. If we knew the best choice to make, we would make that choice. Mistakes are our greatest lessons and become our greatest gifts if we learn from them. Some choices lead us to magnificent success, others lead us to tragic or funny stories. My particular set of choices have left me with some pretty funny stories...and by funny, I mean I have to laugh, otherwise I will cry.

I got sober 4 years prior to this story. I went on an amazing journey to find myself. I thought I did a pretty good job, at least that's what my ego and a handful of people told me! The funny thing is, the more I learned along the way, the less I realized what I actually knew and didn't know! I used to be confused by the saying, the more I learn, the less I know. Now I totally get it. I also love that I actually do know so much more than I ever really understood. Access to the universal consciousness is mind-blowing! The more open I remain, the more magic and miracles I experience daily.

Reflecting back on those years, I can see how I acted like a child. Have you ever seen a little kid that just learned something new? They are so excited; they share it with everyone! They can't wait to show and tell you every detail. At no point does it cross their mind that nothing they are sharing is new to you or that maybe you do not have the time or interest in that moment. They don't care how they are received or even have the awareness to contemplate what being received means. They are just so excited and want to share with the world. Many times, people listen and encourage them, knowing it comes from a place of growth and excitement. Kids will be kids, as the saying goes.

This is great when we are little, however as we age, it stops working so well. When we get sober, or make extreme life changes, we go through this discovery and growth period all over again. The difference is, as adults, we are not so kind and forgiving to each other. As we age, we lose our innocence. We start to see others through our own lenses and judge them based on our own experiences. What was acceptable from an innocent child is not acceptable from an adult. Adults are supposed to know better...

Can you relate? Have you gone through a breakup, loss of a job, recovery, or any life altering experience that left you feeling broken? Have you experienced feeling vulnerable, weak, alone and questioning everything you thought you knew?

Have you wondered if you may be meant to be alone? Have you questioned your purpose? Have you thought, why me? What do I do now?

Have you ever wondered what you are doing wrong? Why is it working for everyone else?

I have. I am right now. Not for the first time. Not for the second time, but for the third time. I have been completely humbled, and the universe is showing me how to rebuild from a place of complete surrender.

I invite you to join me on this quest to deeper love, passion, connection and community. I know I am not alone in the desire to connect and feel like I am part of something bigger than myself. I'll share with you what I learned about how to connect, communicate and be of service without losing myself. I will take you on an intimate journey through my darkest days, vulnerable and hilarious experiences, and real events. Events that were painfully enlightening. Events that may help you see parts of yourself or avoid some of the pain I experienced.

My intention is to show you how much can shift in just over one year. This entire journey took place for me from April to June of the next year. It was a whirlwind fourteen months with twists, turns, tears, and joy that lead me to the ultimate love I was seeking. I can only hope that you may find the answers you seek in my crazy mishaps! Through every mishap, so much wisdom is gained!

Some names and details have been changed to protect identities.

To get the most out of this book, I would suggest getting a journal. There are Opportunity sections at the end of each chapter designed to unlock you as you go. The questions are deliberately asked to open your mind to new perspectives and possibilities. Invest in the process and watch as you discover a path to clarity on who you want to be is unraveled.

You can also find the opportunities, workbook and more support at Groovywillowgreen.com.

NOT AGAIN

April, the year before...

Siting there in the passenger seat, looking out the window with tears streaming down my face, thinking to myself, why? Why didn't you listen to yourself? Why didn't you trust your gut? I thought you were stronger than this? How did you get yourself here again? On a road trip with a man who doesn't know me at all...

As we sat down for our last breakfast before dropping George off at the airport, he looked at me. He looked at me often, however I think this was the first time he actually saw me. As he looked at me across the table, he reflected on what he believed to be our future. In his mind, we were getting married and living happily ever after. As he spoke, I cried harder.

He finally noticed and said, "what happened to you? When we met, you were so bright and alive. Now you are so dark and exhausted." It never once occurred to him that is was him who sucked the light out of me. He was like a vacuum cleaner, a toxic hose that once stuck, was a nightmare to remove.

And as much as I wanted to hate him, I couldn't, because it was me who allowed it. I allowed this person to get too close to me. I ignored the red flags, I ignored my gut, I ignored all the warning signs. This was my real problem. I was disgusted with myself for letting this man in. I was disgusted with myself for going to deep into his illusion. I felt sick, and I couldn't wait to get away.

Once I finally dropped him at the airport, I drove to Susun Weed's where I was set to do an internship. I had come to Susun 3 years ago, when I was only 3 months sober. It was the best decision I ever made. The experience freed me from so many labels, ideas, and opened me up to the possibilities and magic life has to offer.

When the invitation to return opened up, I knew it must be a sign. I also knew going back to New York and getting out of SWFL would allow me to get away from George and the mess I had gotten myself into. It was like Deja Vu returning to Susun's. I was running from another man. I was running to the one place I felt safe. Or so I thought.

Safety, what does that really mean? Think about it. What does safety mean to you? What are you willing to compromise for the idea of safety?

I made time and space to really reflect on that question, along with many others. I asked myself how I got into this mess again! Where did I let myself down? What is this teaching me? I had to get clarity on the choices I made and what the intentions behind those choices were. I had to really look at myself, honestly. I had to be willing to see the truth, my truth.

One of the most useful tools I picked up over the years is reflection, and to challenge myself to learn and understand without judgment. My initial reaction was to blame, first him for not respecting my boundaries and honoring me...then myself for allowing this behavior. However, neither of these options is useful. Blame and forgiveness are such wastes of energy. Without blame, forgiveness is not necessary. It took me a long time to get to this point. To understand that each event is just that, an event. Without it, I would not have learned and grown.

So, I really needed to look at this experience objectively, without emotion or judgement and ask myself, what was I thinking?

What was my intention? Why didn't I listen to my gut? What was I hoping to gain? What was my intention when I chose to override my intuition and get too close to this person?

The answers made me sick... I was bored and desperate for connection. It had been so long since I had been touched. I was finally comfortable in my skin and now I wanted that skin to be touched. I was needy. I wanted to be seen and heard. I wanted to be important. I wanted to make a difference.

Well, like attracts like. I was needy and attracted my perfect mirror. In the beginning he soaked up everything I said. It was amazing, he was learning, growing, expanding. He was hungry to learn. His hunger fed my desire to teach, to give, to lead. It fed me, until it didn't. I was focused on his potential and lost sight of the present reality. The second I allowed the boundaries to be blurred, everything went south...quickly.

He invited me to go to his appointments as he trained dogs. I observed. The more I observed, the more I learned about power and feeling powerless. It's amazing how people, myself included, create realities to take back our power. Or create the perception of taking back our power. I witnessed him projecting his needs onto the animal and ordering the owners to see the dog the way he needed his parents to see him. He was scolding his parents with every session and healing a part of himself in the process. It was a win/win/win on many levels. The owners connected with their dog, the dog was learning boundaries and George was empowering himself.

The moment I gave him the power within our relationship, it was like a bomb went off. I wanted to see what he would do if I completely empowered him. He showed me exactly how he uses it; there was no power, only force. A painful force that almost destroyed me. From that moment forward, I don't believe he ever saw me, heard me or thought about my experience again.

What I experienced was painful. Every conversation, every event was a demand for me to see him, witness him and celebrate him. He no longer honored my boundaries or any part of me. He wanted all the power and the spotlight and was clueless about how much his actions were actually hurting the people he claimed to be loving. We went camping and all he wanted was me to witness what a man he was. He wanted me to witness him using the axe, building the fire, seeing how amazing he was. Honestly, I could have been anyone, he didn't see me. My role was to witness him.

And the sex....WHAT WAS I THINKING????? OMG! It's embarrassing to share; however, I know I am not alone! I was so desperate to be touched that I opened myself up to this man. Wow! Even during sex, he wanted to control me! Imagine this-- (yes, you can laugh)

I have always been very open about the fact that I LOVE foot rubs. I am a sucker for a good foot or back rub. And that is how it all began, he wanted me and made it clear. He knew my desires, and I let him rub my feet. From there, the energy inside me started to lite up, it was working, I was getting turned on. It had been so long, and against all of my better judgment, I allowed it to go too far. My body was feeling alive, loving all the sensations. I was so caught up in the sensations and physical connections I had been longing for, I completely lost all sense of my brain and just surrendered to the moment, only to be jerked back to reality as he aggressively was in my face, saying; "Open your eyes. Look at me. Look at me NOW!" You can imagine my shock and disbelief. I was dumbfounded and so disappointed with myself. I was open to an experience, but I need to practice better discernment on who to share the experiences with! He didn't care about me!

I had never experienced that before! Granted, I haven't really had a healthy sex life. This is all new to me...and how else am I going to learn. However, I knew this is definitely not what I wanted!

I allowed this one more time. We had talked about the prior attempt and I thought we had an understanding. I believed he understood that if we are going to connect, there needed to be a mutual respect, allowing us each to have our own experience with each other. It's a co-creation, not dictation! It was the weekend we went camping. I thought "what is more romantic than making love under the stars"? I had already let him in, I was open to the option of it working. So, we attempted to make love one more time. He never opened his eyes. There was no demand I look at him. Instead, I think I could have been a blow-up doll. Just like the rest of the camping experience, it was pretty much him putting on a show and I was just there to witness. He had an entire experience from beginning to climax, never once being present or conscious of the fact that it was not a co-creation. He finished and was so proud of himself, clueless that I was laying there in disgust with myself and sick to my stomach watching him.

I felt so gross! I knew I needed to get away. I knew I needed to end this relationship, however, I had no idea how. He was so aggressive and did not care what I said. He was convinced we were getting married, and did not care that I was not even close to happy. I would sit there and cry and he would talk about our future...he couldn't even see me. All he saw was his fantasy and I was the object that he decided was the one to fulfill it with. Like I said, I could have been a blow-up doll holding space in his fantasy world. What on earth was I doing? Was I really this desperate? I wanted to puke. I did puke.

Again, why did I allow this man to suck the life force out of me? Why did I give away my power? What was my intention, expectation, weakness?

Does any of this sound familiar? Have you found yourself going down a path you know you shouldn't, yet you just can't stop yourself? And then you reach the end and wonder how you got here, again?

Reflection

I learned that when I am feeling bored, weak or lonely... I need to sit with those feelings. This is the best time to discover more ways to love myself and the absolute worst time to date or even consider a relationship! This is an opportunity to find clarity and ask myself, what do I want? What is my purpose?

When I look back at how I allowed the relationship to go too far, I had to acknowledge some really hard truths about myself. I was happy being alone. Then I got bored and wanted to help someone else. I allowed my desires to get in the way of helping him. I can totally see how I created more havoc than healing by not standing my ground. I knew better than to get to close to this person. I could see his inner child demanding attention. I could see that to best serve him, I should hold that space with love and not allow him to bully and manipulate me. I see how I actually failed him and myself.

I allowed my desire to be touched and to experience love to cloud my choices. This didn't honor me or him. I knew better. So how can I do it better next time? Stay firm and set hard boundaries. Honor the boundaries and trust my gut. Honor my body.

I remind myself that I am happier alone. I don't need to settle to feel loved. I am worthy of love, respect, and being seen.

We teach people how to treat us by how we treat ourselves, what we accept and what we allow.

George helped me understand what it feels like not to be seen or heard. He was trapped in his own delusion; he never saw me.

It's time for me to raise the bar!

What about you?

Is any of this resonating with you?

Have you allowed yourself to go too far and then wondered how in the heck did I get here?

You are not alone!!!

Opportunity

I allowed this to happen because I wasn't prepared for when I was bored. I had always been doing something. So let's prepare you for those moments you feel scared, lonely, bored or just need something constructive to do.

What are you passionate about?

What do you dream about?

What makes you feel alive?

Write about it. Write out all the things you love doing, big and small.

Next I want you to think about safety, or security. What does that mean to you?

What do you think you need? Really think about this. Look over your list and ask yourself, is this a need or a want? Am I willing to compromise my dreams for this? Am I willing to compromise my freedom for this? How can I provide it for myself, or can I live without it?

TRUST YOUR GUT

April

Have you ever gone back to a place in your childhood, the playground you were on, the hill you used to think was huge, or some other happy place you remember? Not just remember, but have vivid memories? You can go back to the joy and laughter of the event and feel it. You can see the magnitude this experience had on you as a child, only to realize as an adult, it's nothing like you remember!

This was my experience with Susun. I spent over 3 months living with her, learning, growing, getting deprogrammed. It took me a couple of years to really unpack what I learned from the experience. I showed up 3 months sober, experiencing brain fog after coming off 25 years of pharmaceuticals, and I was terrified of life. I was at a loss. My hopelessness and desperation allowed me to show up fully, I had nothing to lose. I completely surrendered to the experience. And at the time, it was the absolute best thing for me. I learned so much. I honestly believed at the time I had fully stepped into my power! Looking back, I laugh. I now see the more power I thought I had, the less I actually did. It was a long road discovering the difference between power and force. I had to practice. I sat and listened. I listened to the guidance I was receiving. I created a language with my guides, one that I committed to mastering. I dedicate time and space to strengthening it daily and have not missed a day since 2015. The investment has changed my life.

I was so excited to return Susun's for round two. I had such a tremendous breakthrough the first time that I put her on a pedestal. I couldn't wait to see what I would learn this time. This time, however, I saw the woman with new eyes.

Long story short, I quickly realized that nothing was as it seemed. The experience I remembered was definitely the same, only very different. Susun was still Susun, she taught through screaming and swearing. I remember it well! I will never forget one of the most impactful lessons I gained from Susun.

One morning I shared, "I apologized for being a bitch in advance, because I did not sleep well."

She glared at me and said "FUCK YOU!"

I was shocked. I was caught off guard. "What are you talking about?"

Susun replied, "Why would you say that?"

Me, "My mom says I'm a bitch when I'm tired.'

Susun, "Guess what? Mommy isn't here. And you have a choice, do you want to be a bitch?"

Me, "No."

Susun, "Then walk over there, meditate for 5 minutes and come back with a new attitude. However, if you do decide you want to be a bitch, that's ok, as long as you own it. If you chose to be a bitch, look at me and tell me you are being a bitch because you want to, and own your attitude."

Holy shit that was powerful. I hugged her. I had no idea how powerless I acted.

Her aggressiveness didn't faze me so much the first time around. I felt so liberated and free. Fuck just seemed to be part of the regular vocabulary around there. I had no idea the impact this all had on me until I left...

Over the years, I got feedback that I was rather aggressive and abrasive. I was bluntly honest and to the point. I didn't really worry about how I was received as much as I worried about being honest and powerful. I took on a lot of Susun's traits. I needed that shock value and smack to the head to wake up and get present! I was never present prior to Susun. I assumed that everyone else needed that same wake up call. I didn't understand that you can teach someone to be present through love, compassion and kindness.

Round two was very different. The aggressiveness no longer felt good. I was exhausted. I wanted to learn, however, I no longer needed the screaming and aggression in order to hear. I was there to listen, to serve, to learn. I understood my role and that she would need to yell at me in front of the newbies so I could model the response. However, I asked her for softer and gentler this time. I expressed that I was ready to learn through love, joy, and laughter. I was willing to play the required role for my internship agreement, however when no one else was around, I needed a different relationship. Susun taught me to ask for exactly what I needed, and I did. I needed the verbal aggressiveness to stop. I needed conversations in a respectful and mindful tone. I needed respect. I made my needs very clear. I communicated to Susun exactly as she had taught me. I shared that the aggressive and abrasive behavior was actually making me sick and bringing back suicidal thoughts.

The screaming continued. Have you ever watched those movies, the ones where the protesters are standing there silently while the cops in full raid gear do everything they can to provoke them? The cops antagonize the person, hoping they will move so they can arrest them. That is what I felt like. When I didn't weed the plants correctly, or picked the wrong thing, Susun would get right up in my face, less than 6 inches from my ear and scream, 'You fucking murderer! You..."

And if I spoke, it would just get worse. I was allowed one response, "I hear you Susun, thank you."

In the moment, this was painful, so painful. Looking back, it was such a valuable experience. She knew I came from an abusive relationship with a narcissist that used to gaslight me. I was the perfect victim and he the perfect abuser. She was training me to not allow my emotions to be triggered. In her way, she was LOVING me and preparing me for battle. She gave me one of the greatest gifts... however, I could only take so much. I needed to experience love too. The first time around, I felt that love. I felt the love as deeply as the aggression and pain.

The second time around, everything was different. I can speculate, however that honors no one. What I can say is that I struggled for more than 2 weeks before deciding to leave early. I had been setting my intentions daily, asking to learn through love, laughter, and joy. I was done learning through pain and suffering. I spent 40 years in the dark! I was comfortable there. I was ready to experience love. I knew love started with me, and what I was experiencing was no longer acceptable to me. I had given my word that I would stay for an agreed amount of time and my word was all I had. If I were going to leave early, something big had to happen.

I pulled tarot cards every morning and meditated. I was getting very clear messages that it was time to go. Everything inside me and out was saying LEAVE NOW. Yet, I couldn't. I felt obligated to stay, for many reasons beyond just my word. I respected this woman and wanted to honor our agreement and I knew she needed help. Yet every time I asked her to back off and lighten up, the aggressiveness got worse. My messages where coming stronger and stronger. I asked for an undeniable sign. I needed to know that if I left early, it was absolutely for my best interest.

In less than 24 hours I got that sign. An angel appeared. A magical angel that witnessed what I was experiencing, admired Susun as much as I do, and wanted to help me. This angel was truly a gift from the heavens. She filled me with light, love and clarity. Though I did not know why I needed to leave, and leave quickly, I did. I asked for help and I trusted the answer that made no sense to me at the time. Within a week of leaving, everything was revealed to me. I was saved from being part of a huge fiasco.

My guides were leading me on the path of least resistance and to safety. My intuition was dead on. This was a huge opportunity for me to learn to trust fully. Trust my gut when absolutely nothing else makes sense. When I set my intentions to learn though love, joy and laughter...that is exactly where my guides where taking me. It took a bit to get there, however I was well on my way.

Reflection

Susun opened me up to choices. She taught me to never be a victim again, to stand in my power. She trained me to not allow my emotions to get the better of me. She taught me the power of controlling emotions and witnessing events. She taught me discernment. She showed me extremes. She taught me honor. She taught me the power of honesty and integrity over being liked. She models staying on your path no matter what. She opened my eyes to so many things. The contrast of returning showed me where I was and solidified where I was going. There was no question I was ready for light, love, laughter and joy.

I also learned the difference between worshiping the message vs the messenger.

The wake-up calls and messages are everywhere. I was stuck idolizing the messenger rather than understanding that the messages are freely available to all. I have seen this in others as well, we hear the voice that freed us loudest and honor it as Truth. In reality this does not honor you are the messenger. Finding your own Truth and living it does.

Opportunity

I was so grateful to Susun that I never questioned her the first time I was there. She was the teacher I chose and the person that helped me see. I put her on a pedestal. This wasn't fair to her or me. Since then, I have met many people who share the same wisdom. I have learned that the information is there, presented in many forms. There are many teachers, many masters and many ways to share knowledge. We all have access and it boils down to trusting yourself above all. Are there teachers in your life you give your power to?

How are the people you choose to learn from empowering you?

What are you learning that strengthens your ability to trust yourself?

Pinpoint and list times in your life that you trusted yourself, even when it didn't make sense.

Pinpoint and list the times you may not have, and then kicked yourself.

Compare the differences. Look at the outcomes. Looking at both, make a list of the times you did trust your gut. Then make a list of how grateful you were. Keep this list somewhere you can access it regularly to remind you to trust yourself!

INTENTIONS AND REFLECTIONS

May

It's pretty awesome how things always seem to come back full circle. The first time I was at Susun's I met this amazing woman, I will call her Alice, whom I have stayed connected with over the years. She works for Susun and was part of the reason I returned. She and another one on Susun's closest allies both asked me to come.

Alice chose to live with Susun the summer after I did. The experience of living there is something that cannot be explained, therefore the bond that forms between the women who survive it is pretty strong. Think of soldiers returning from war; they witnessed things that people who have not been on the battle field can comprehend. And many don't want to, they are just happy to have their freedom. This is the type of bond that forms at Susun's. The things we witness and experience are intense, mind-blowing and hard to explain. It's a world that many will never experience and most who do choose not to stay and fully understand. Many women do not ever finish their commitment, actually less than 25% finish. The training is hard. The experience involves a lot of screaming, aggressiveness, and darkness. Susun holds a space that is huge, which can be both very healing and very detrimental. The first time around, it was exactly what I needed to wake up. I was not present in my body. I was overrun with labels. I had brain fog, was freshly sober, not just from alcohol, but from an Adderall / Xanax cycle as well. I needed a harsh wake up call.

I was so excited about all my breakthroughs, I encouraged women to come learn from Susun. I encouraged Alice to Apprentice. She did. I was available as her support. She had an equally life altering experience. She works for her still and was one of the biggest catalysts getting me back to New York. She was also one of the biggest advocates for me to leave early. She witnessed the new me and the new relationship this created with Susun.

She heard me when I said, I no longer need aggression. I am ready to live, learn and experience light, love, joy and laughter.

It was with her that I discussed and debated my early departure and the experiences leading me to those thoughts. It was important to me to honor and respect Susun, she was one of my greatest teachers, mentors, and inspirations. Again, only the women who have lived there understand and have felt the love that is equal to the pain. Despite the aggressive, abusive behavior, there is no question in my mind that Susun also loves, protects, and honors those she adores, equally and intensely. Alice also knew this side of Susun.

Alice and her husband, Ralph had recently purchased a house and invited me to come stay with them for a while. They had some work that they wanted done and needed some help. Alice also hired me to do some of my magic on her, her new home, and with her family. She was familiar with my medicine and success with the clients I had worked with. I agreed and went to stay with her for a while.

It was the perfect opportunity for me to catch my balance, reflect and reboot while helping friends. The plan was for me to stay for a few months and help them really make some shifts.

The deal was I was would do body work, energy sessions and ceremonial work for Alice, and the home. I was also asked to oversee contractors for some upgrades. Alice and Ralph were both introverts and didn't like dealing with people. They had so much resistance to talking with strangers they had been putting off upgrades to their house. So, they hired me to make the contact and oversee some remodeling as well as build some pieces for their house. We were all excited for the journey. I had a place to heal and be of service at the same time. Ralph and Alice were excited they had someone to make their dreams a reality.

In order to best serve Alice and Ralph, I needed clarity. Clarity on what just happened and how to let it go and heal. Clarity on the timeline and expectations, and clarity on what was next.

I needed to be clear, alert and fully present to do the work I committed to do. I needed to really sit and reflect on my experience. I had to answer the tough questions.

How did you get here? What did you learn? What did you expect? How was this different?

What do you want now? What needs to shift?

Have you ever asked yourself these questions? We are creators of our experiences. I really needed to figure out how I manifested this and how to manifest the joy I wanted to experience.

So that is exactly what I did. I invited Alice to do the same. In order for me to serve her, I needed clarity on what she wanted to experience and her expectations of what that looked like.

I spent some time alone, meditating. I remembered my journals, my intentions. I had been journaling and setting intentions for about 3 years. I was getting better and better at the process.

I had been using techniques I learned from my friend Tony Burroughs and his book Intenders of the Highest Good. I looked back through all my intentions, meditations and notes from messages I'd received.

One of my strongest messages was that I am here to learn and share truth. I had no idea what that meant; however, I had been on a mission to figure it out! What I learned was each individual perception is its own truth to the one perceiving it. My truth is only from my perception. I create my reality through the story I tell and the words I use. I figured out that I can rewrite my reality with each thought, each belief, each choice and each action. Tell a new story and the entire experience changes. The more perspectives I can see, the more information I had to upgrade my story. I had been studying and mastering how to rewrite my reality to become the life that I want. So, I went to my notes to see exactly how I created this reality.

How did the words actually manifest? How was it exactly what I asked for? How did I expect it to look? What did I really create?

I had to look at myself, take full responsibility for my choices and see what I could learn. This is not easy. It can be painful to look back and realize that my choices, my decisions, my fears are exactly what created my pain. However, the willingness to look at, and to feel the pain creates the path to freedom and something different!

So, after reflecting, I decided to focus on where I wanted to go from here. I created an outline, highlighting what I wanted to experience. I then gave Alice a copy and encouraged her to do the same. This exercise worked so well for both of us that I have used is with many clients!

Here is a copy of what I created, a basic outline of what I wanted my life to look like in that moment.

I. Space Needs

A. I own the land and can keep it sacred/protected/safe

B. 10 acres+

C. trees/woods

D. water that people can be submerged in

E. art studio space

F. yoga/meditation space

G. personal living space

H. space for clients to stay

I. kitchen for group cooking and additional space separate from my personal area

II. Personal Needs

A. Sacred time for self-care

a. Massage

b. Yoga

c. Meditation

d. Creativity

e. Writing

B. Confidant to process/talk/work through my "stuff"

C. Long walks

D. Love and Laughter

E. Travel

F. Videos/Round talks/Mastermind opportunities

G. Infusion and proper nourishment

III. Professional Support Needs

A. Promotion/Advertising

B. Selling/Closing/Seeing and Creating the Value to others

C. Handling details/money/supplies/Day to day stuff

    D. Technical support

        a. Email Marketing

        b. Website

        c. Videos

            □ Weekly, YouTube posts

            □ Add intro/ending/graphics

IV. Lover Needs

    A. Sees my passion, understands my needs and encourages them

    B. Understands my strengths and encourages them

        a. Manifesting

        b. Making things happen

        c. Creating community

        d. Working in the cosmic realm

    C. Understands my challenges and Communicates with me on what needs to be done

        a. Handling money

        b. Handling details

    D. Chemistry/Passion

        a. Soft and Gentle

        b. Wants to explore what turns me on and how I receive

        c. Enjoys rubbing my back, feet, body

        d. Enjoys physical touch, hugging, holding hands, cuddling

        e. Romantic getaways and dates

V. Services I offer

A. Rituals

B. Ceremonies

    a. Weddings

    b. Birthdays

    c. End of Life Celebrations

    d. Anniversaries

    e. Medicinal

C. Community events

    a. Moon Celebrations

       ☐ New

       ☐ Full

    b. Solstice events

       ☐ Winter

       ☐ Summer

    c. Equinoxes

       ☐ Spring

       ☐ Autumn

    d. Healing Circles

       ☐ Moon Lodge (Women Only)

       ☐ Meditation

       ☐ Drum

       ☐ Dance

    e. Workshops

       ☐ Find your voice

□ Self-Nourishment

- Physical

- Mental

- Emotional

- Spiritual

□ Plant Medicine

□ Artistic Expression

D. Retreats

a. Relaxing

b. Self-Empowerment

c. Spiritual Journey

d. Medicinal

E. Paid to travel and do retreats

I then reflected on the intentions I wrote that got me where I was, then refined them.

Here is what I had asked for and how it manifested.

I intend I see both light and dark with clarity. I was seeing contrast everywhere. When I speak of this contrast of light and dark, I am speaking in terms of alignment, good/bad, what feeds the light and love, and what feeds the darkness or pain. I wanted to understand, and to understand means I have to experience the pain and contrast. I was indeed experiencing many contradictions, contrast, and pain. The clarity was exactly what I both wanted and needed.

I am now ready to let go of the darkness and enter into the light.

I live in the perfect harmony, surrounded with love, supporting me physically, emotionally, spiritually, financially. I live in perfect harmony both within and without. I am abundant with resources, love, energy, laughter and peace, always having plenty to use, plenty to share and plenty to spare. I am surrounded with people who have integrity. I am surrounded and supported by a community of others who love life, laughter, and enjoy the moment. I feel connected to the people closest to me. I have a loving, supportive, core group of friends that are like family. We give each other the benefit of the doubt, have each other's backs, love, honor and respect each other. My core group protects each other and sees the highest view. We hold each other to a high standard with love, compassion and acceptance. We speak highly of each other, promoting, loving and co-creating growth.

The clarity and contrast were exactly what I asked for. In my mind, I expected love and community, in reality I got the opposite. This was the perfect opportunity for me to clarify what I had experienced and what I want to experience next. I was willing to see where I was out of alignment, how I got there, then redirect. To honor the intention I put out there, things had to shift. The universe was aligning me with what I asked for. Every shift, every transition takes time to realign. I was now very conscious that I was experiencing what I asked for. My intention to live, learn, and experience joy was new. I had not asked for that before. The new direction will take a few shifts to realign my experiences to match.

Next, I looked at LOVE. This was one of my deepest desires. I wanted to experience true love, true connection with my partner. So, I set my new intentions...

I intend I see my path unfolding easily and effortlessly in front of me. I intend I always know the next best move quickly and intuitively respond with grace and ease. I intend I am a lighthouse, a source of power, with love and integrity. I intend I am in perfect union with my higher self and the universe as spirit works through me. I intend my medicine is sought after, recognized and respected. I intend I am compensated generously, easily, and effortlessly. I AM TRUTH. Truth sets people free.

I AM LOVE. Love opens hearts and restores hope, faith, and Trust. I am clairvoyant and clairaudient. I intend to have all the resources I need, they come to me easily and effortlessly in abundance, with plenty to use, plenty to spare, and plenty to share. I intend all resources show up easily and effortlessly in abundance before I know they are necessary.

I intend I align with the perfect property to share my gifts, be steward of the land and live in harmony as it comes to me easily and effortlessly. I intend I live a life filled with joy, laughter, love and abundance.

I intend I align with my male partner seamlessly and effortlessly, with love, joy, abundance, passion, and grace. I intend to get swept up in LOVE and bring out the best of myself and others, with love, honor, compassion and support. May this partner have blue eyes, intelligence, and grace. I intend we laugh often and bring out the best in one another, love and support each other and help each other grow.

I intend I live harmoniously, and always have the means, power, clarity, and willingness to expand, travel, and grow, creating a life more abundant and magical than I could comprehend at this time. I intend I am honored; my body, mind, spirit, soul, and my medicine. I intend to be seen and heard, laugh often, and allow my inner child to play. I intend to see both light and dark with clarity. I intend I see both light and dark with compassion and grace. I intend my life be filled with experiences, people, opportunities, love, laughter and abundance on a scale bigger than I could possibly comprehend in this moment. I intend I am guarded, guided and protected at all times. I AM Happy, Healthy and Whole. I intend all is for the highest and greatest good of everyone, everywhere, the universe and myself. So, Mote it be.

I set my intentions and let go. Now it's time to trust and flow with what is being delivered to me. I asked for a world, experiences, people, places and opportunities that were bigger than my mind could comprehend, and that were beyond my ability to ask for. I asked to be guided to the people, places, and experiences I did not know how to ask for... so now I just needed to be open to receive.

For guidance, I would do my yoga, meditation and daily card readings in the morning. The I would trust the instincts I got and follow them. My instincts lead me to Jay Street in Schenectady, NY where I met an Angel! I wandered into Crossroads Gifts & Wellness. It was like home. The energy felt magical and pure. They had crystals, magic, books, and so much more. One corner caught my eyes immediately, a book exchange! I love books! I sat on the floor and started looking through the options. There were several that I was interested in. I wandered up to the counter and asked about the exchange. I pulled out a copy of my first book, "I'm Sober, Now What? Moving through the fear, anxiety and Humility of LIFE, on Life's terms." and asked if I could exchange it. Lis, the owner agreed. She then asked where I got the book, she was interested in selling them!

That was the beginning of the universal shift for me. Lis was my angel. Lis was the beginning of a paradigm shift and the universe showing me a new way of being, of living, of loving. When I told Lis I wrote the book and would be happy to put some in her store, she agreed to purchase several.

From there we talked about the retreats, workshops and services I offer. We started planning workshops and talking about all the possibilities. The planning had begun! I was so excited!

Meanwhile...

I heard from a man we will call Henry, a blue-eyed man that had been in and out of my life. I met him when I was newly sober and we dated some. We went back and forth for about 3 years. I had strong feelings for him when we spent time together. I believed he cared about me too, however, I knew it was important to him that I find myself and get clear on me.

He wasn't the commitment type, nor did he like needy and lost women! We had different intentions about the future and what we wanted from each other. They didn't align. I hadn't seen or talked to him in months.

He wanted to reconnect. I wasn't sure of his intentions; however, I was prepared to take full responsibility for my future and what I wanted. Henry had asked to come see me, he talked about us going to see his friend Daniel in Costa Rica. He has talked about Daniel's retreat center in the past. Henry knew my desire to hold retreats and create events. Henry also shared that he thought I would love Daniel's and the experience. He thought we should go!

This all sounded great! It felt like the universe was aligning everything I asked for seamlessly, as requested. I was open to the idea of exploring where this may go.... I was open to reconnecting with Henry. I was hopeful that maybe after 3 years, we may finally align and there could be a future!

Henry asked me where I was and offered to fly anywhere to see me. I talked to Alice and Ralph. They opened their home and were excited to meet Henry. They were excited for me that the universe seemed to be delivering me all the magic and opportunities I had asked for.

After talking with Henry, I wanted to make it clear what my intentions were, given our past. I loved this man. We had a history. I didn't want to leave room for confusion. I sent him a 2-page letter, expressing to him all the things I love and value about him, our friendship, and who he has been in my life. I also shared that I am clear on what I want and where I am going. I included my outline, my future and what I wanted. I shared with Henry that this is what I am working toward and asked that he please be honest with me. If he could see himself in that role, the lover, the partner, and if my desires made sense and he aligned with my vision, please come! If not, if he did not see himself able to support my dreams, or if he really didn't have any interest in where I want to go, and opening his heart and life to the possibilities, then please do not come. Please leave me alone and let me find my way.

Henry received the letter, acknowledged the letter and still wanted to come to New York and see me. He still wanted to move forward with our trip to Costa Rica and he expressed that he was open to seeing where it all goes.

Alice was excited for all the opportunities opening up for me. We established a timeline about two months out, at the end of which my mom was going to join me for the next leg of my journey. Don, my stepfather, was ill, so for her to set up being able to join me took some planning. We set a date and she bought a plane ticket.

Once she flew to meet me, we were going to drive through Canada to Michigan to visit family, then visit other friends on the way back to Florida where I would reconnect with Henry.

I was so excited... I believed that the universe was aligning magically!

Reflections

Are you deliberately creating your reality or are you allowing life to happen to you?

No choice, is an actual choice.

Let me repeat that,

No choice is a choice.

The inability to decide, or to be resistance to deliberate creation, is a powerful choice to not take responsibility for our experiences. Choosing to not reflect on how you got where you are will guarantee no change. Don't wait for the fear of staying the same to motivate you to move through the fear of looking at yourself and creating deliberate change.

Opportunity

How clear are you on what you want?

Use the templet below and write about each category. Make lists.

1. Space needs/or total freedom of space

2. Personal Needs/Self care

3. Professional desires

4. Lover/partnership/family/community

5. Services

6. Anything else that you want to add

Next, set your intentions. Write out in detail what the experience feels and looks like. If you're not sure, go broad and get more detailed as you go. Write what feels good. Don't worry about how, just focus on what comes easy. Allow yourself to get lost in the fantasy as you go. You can always come back, add more, or rewrite it as it unfolds.

Write in present tense. Avoid words like wishing, trying, hoping, and wanting. Instead use creating, doing, living. Write your intentions and story as if you are living it. Feel yourself experiencing it as you write. Allow yourself to get lost in your daydream.

RECEIVING THE MESSAGES

June

Among the services Alice requested from me was ceremonial work and helping her establish a language with her guides. It's important to understand how we receive guidance and that we each receive differently. The universe speaks, guides, opens doors and shines light on our path. The signals are there. The question is, are you receiving the messages? Do you understand how you're being guided? It is possible to create your own language. By deliberately creating the language in which you wish to receive, it makes it easier to get the messages and avoid misunderstandings. I receive through numbers, symbolism, feeling, and just a sense of knowing. I work daily to strengthen my internal compass. She wanted help understanding hers and getting clarity.

I had just revisited my intentions and reset them. I invited her to do the same. To open up the portal, clarity was essential. We were both crystal clear on what direction we wanted to go.

I was clear about wanting to transition into experiencing life filled with much more love, joy and laughter. This for me meant an entire paradigm shift. I had mostly experienced pain and suffering. I was surrounded with people who embraced the darkness and pain, it was the only home I knew. I said I was willing to go through as much pain as necessary to move through this transition as quickly and swiftly as possible. I wanted to get to the other side. I was done suffering and ready to walk in the light. I desperately wanted change. Love, joy, and laughter were my new path. I was familiar with the process. Shifting is like riding a motorcycle really fast. If you want to change directions, you need to do it gradually. I was willing to scrape a knee to turn sharper and faster!

Alice was clear that she wanted to stay in the darkness, that she had no intentions of shifting. When I do ceremonial work, I end every ceremony intending the highest and greatest good of everyone, everywhere, the universe and myself, with harm to none, so mote it be. She didn't want me using good or light. She demanded I find another way. I knew we were in for a shift and would be moving in different directions from this point forward.

I found a way to honor both my commitment to her as well as my commitment to only create ceremonies supporting the highest light of all and harm to none.

I created several ceremonies to support her new home, each of our individual intentions, and to honor our decisions on the paths we desire.

I work with the elements, the seven directions, and inspiration fromthe writings and teachings of various cultural myths and legends. Much of my inspiration has been of Egyptian decent. The first was Bassett, then Thoth, Osiris and Ma'at. Thoth represents Wisdom while Ma'at symbolizes Truth, Justice, and Cosmic Order. I've received impressions patterned after Ma'at's teachings in visions both asleep and awake. Her guidance was priceless.

One of the messages I received was to follow the red feather, the feather of Truth. It will always guide you home. The message was powerful and I wasn't sure what to take from it. I could feel a shift was coming. After Alice and I finished this ceremony, I felt a heaviness start to sink in. A heaviness I have felt before. I had no idea what was about to happen, I just kept hearing, 'follow the red feather, it will guide you home.' I have learned to trust my instincts and the messages I receive. I could feel I was about to go for an intense ride, so I tattooed the red feather on my arm to remind me.

This was the beginning of the change in our relationship. She made it very clear, my joy and love were not welcome. She enjoyed the suffering and the struggle. She went to Susun's on weekends to work and returned with more rage every time. She was making a conscious choice to do this. I know this because we talked about it. I had all kinds of visions and offered to shine light on a way to free her from this cycle. She declined; she didn't want to see it. She chose not to see her blind spots and was unwilling to explore any new options. She told me she was too scared to see and just not ready.

I had no choice. To honor all meant I could not free her without permission. I had to honor the path she chose for herself, it's her life.

Reflections

Are you conscious of the messages you are receiving? I really trust myself, my messages and honor my path. I also had to really honor Alice's free will and choice to stay stuck. It was not easy to watch her choose to suffer. I wanted desperately to free her, however I couldn't. I had to respect her choice. I had to love myself enough to also respect my own. I had to let go and continue to follow my path, the one towards love. I made a very conscious choice to choose love above all. Letting Others Voluntarily Evolve.

By choosing not to face a fear, you are creating by default. Default patterns, thoughts, beliefs and behaviors will continue the cycle until broken.

Opportunities

How do you receive messages and guidance?

Do you listen, trust and honor the messages you receive?

What are you afraid of or afraid to see? Hear? Feel?

What do you think will happen if you face the fear?

How would changing your perspective change your reality?

Are you willing to look at yourself and take responsibility for your feelings, reality, experiences and what you are deliberately creating?

Is there a part of you that enjoys the rage, pain and suffering?

What are you gaining from holding on to that suffering? How is it serving you?

What else can you do to achieve these same results?

Where in your life do you consciously go into situations that you know create pain?

What would happen if you chose not to go?

OPEN TO POSSIBILITIES

July

Opportunity comes in the most unexpected and amazing ways. I was introduced to Michael, a master carpenter/builder that lived in Tupper Lake, NY. That was only three hours away from Alice and Ralph's home in the Adirondack Mountains. I had heard this area was amazing, however I had never been. He needed some help chopping wood for the winter and I wanted to build a bench. He agreed to the exchange and said I could come stay with him for the three weeks we thought it would take to get it done. Everything was unfolding better than I could have asked for.

I coordinated with contractors to continue working in my absence. I packed up and headed North to Tupper Lake. The views were breathtaking. The fresh air was intoxicating and healing.

One of the traits I was working on mastering was the art of surrendering to the process and the flow of life. To ask the universe for experiences that were beyond my current comprehension meant I had to be open, without any expectations of what the experience looked like or how it showed up. I was on a journey of complete surrender and willingness to show up, to do my best and see what unfolded.

While working at Michael's I met his dad, Jim, an 89-year-old native of Tupper Lake. He was the gift that opened up a whole new world for me. Jim was a wealth of knowledge, he had so much to share. I was open to hearing it all. I believe he is the real reason I was called to Tupper Lake.

Jim and I started spending every day together. He showed me the area, the history, the beauty of Tupper Lake. He took me on several hikes. Together we hiked to the top of five different mountains. He helped me earn a badge for hiking the Tupper Lake Triad and explained how children and adults come to learn about the mountains. Next, we hiked some bigger mountains and he shared with me how people come back annually to hike all 46 and become part of the Adirondack 46ers club! The magic of the mountains, the hikes, the community, it was more than I could have asked for, better than I could have created. Jim opened me up to the magic that I had only heard about, the magic of the Adirondack Mountains. Each hike was a separate adventure. Each mountain had its own unique energy, views, and healing qualities. For me anything in nature was healing. There is no question that Jim was the real reason I was called to Tupper Lake. I was experiencing connection, joy and beauty on a level beyond what I knew possible. I was in heaven and it just kept getting better!

I met many more people who impacted my visit and taught me so much about what community really is. There was Cassie, this beautiful young woman who hand carves spoons out of wood. She carved me a spoon out of Willow and offered it to me as a gift to nourish myself. She nourishes and loves in a way that is subtle, kind, generous, and heartwarming. Cassie introduced me to Blue Mountain Lake and Castle Rock. We took kayaks across the lake to a trail, a trail you wouldn't find without a local or a guide. We pulled them on shore and then hiked to the top of Castle Rock. It's about a mile, mile and a half hike up. At the top, was a huge rock overlooking the lake and mountains. We simply sat. The views were breathtaking. The company beautiful. I got to know Cassie and how she sees the world, her perspectives, experiences, hopes and dreams. During a dinner party I was able to witness all the ways she connects to her community and family. The experience was precious.

Cassie offered puppet shows at one of the local restaurants, The Tupper Lake Health Hub. This little gem quickly became my favorite place to eat. They have an organic farmers buffet, kombucha on tap, fresh smoothies, organic produce from their farm, amazing grab and go deli salads, fresh and dried herbs, puppet shows for the kids, live folk music, homemade toys, and a community gathering space. This family owned eatery welcomes all. It is a great place to go, enjoy the Adirondack outdoor seating, let your kids run and play with all the others in the huge yard off the deck, or just enjoy a great meal with some wonderful guests.

I had the pleasure of sitting down with the owner, Cherie. Cherie is an extremely humble woman who shared a little of her story with me. About six years ago, Cherie was persuaded to join a farmer's market. She was skeptical, however the demand for organic produce was rising in what she referred to as a food desert. She took the plunge, opened a booth, and met the demand. From there, spirit has guided her and she has listened. The journey evolved into the organic farm to table buffet, market, and community that it is today.

"I call it an eatery, not a restaurant because I want it to be casual" Cherie told me. She really goes out of her way to tell all the guests about the food, the ingredients, and answer any questions they may have. Cherie is conscious of all food sensitivities, restrictions, and personal decisions. She makes all the food on site and provides an array of options to accommodate all dietary choices. And I must say, the real, home cooked food is absolutely tasty!

Cherie also offers a number of desserts. She loves to offer people the mystery dessert. This is a dessert that seems very much like an apple cobbler or pastry dessert that tastes wonderful, however, it's not apple. She offers a prize to anyone who can guess the mystery ingredient. So far, many have guessed, but only few have correctly named the mystery main ingredient. Either way, it is one to satisfy the taste buds!

I spent many nights at the Hub sharing meals with Jim, Cassie, and many other locals I had the pleasure to meet. Each touched my heart and impacted me in a very special way. Some I met at the local meetings and recovery center where I was invited to share my story, others I met on the mountain, and then there were those I just met through divine intervention. I sat with them, enjoyed meals with them. We shared stories, I learned about where they came from and who they are. Some even took me on a mini adventure, showing me what they cherish. One of my favorite adventures was being invited to a field for a fire and to star gaze. We had no idea it was the night of a meteor shower. It was cold, however as the meteors started flowing, we deiced the darkness was more important than the warmth of the fire. We ended up cuddling up with blankets and watching a meteor shower from the back of a pickup truck. I felt like I was in a country music video with great company and an open sky in the middle of nowhere. The movie in the sky was one of the best movies I have ever seen.

There was so much open space. So many places to explore. Luckily Jim's son, Robert, owner of Raquette River Outfitters was able to offer even more insight to the area. His knowledge of the area was expansive and I really appreciated him letting us use kayaks, canoes, bikes and whatever we needed to explore. However, what impacted me the most was his love and commitment to his family, friends, community and showing guests the area. He offers so much to his guests to assist them in having the best vacation or experience they desire. He also has dinner with his staff, his family, his community. Robert appreciates his team and lets them know how important they are. He does all this with his partner Anne, who is an absolute blessing and welcoming treasure. Together they really go above and beyond. It was beautiful to witness and be a part of.

I was also invited to one of Jim's family dinners at his sister's house where I got to meet even more of this huge and amazing family. Again, I was living the life I asked for. Community, inclusion, connection and love. I was truly experiencing everything I asked for, only in no way I could have predicted. I was open to receiving and the universe was delivering.

Reflections

I chose to surrender and trust my gut to guide me. I trusted my intuition and went for a ride, knowing the universe was answering my intentions.

Cherie was a perfect example of this. She listened to the call of the universe to start a stand at the farmer's market. She was willing to move into the unknown, through the fear. She pushed through the resistance and trusted what she was being called to do. From there she trusted and went with the flow, growing into this amazing space, fully supported and loved by the community. She created space for her kids to grow and others to become a part of something bigger than themselves. She was open, and followed the signs. The community she has created is welcoming, loving, thriving and I feel blessed to have experienced it.

Opportunities

What expectations are you willing to let go of to allow yourself to be open to ways that are more magical than you could have created on your own?

How can you surrender and allow all that you desire to come to you?

What possibilities are opening up for you?

How can you trust the process?

LETTING GO

August

As my time at Tupper Lake was nearing the end, I was in a place of needing nothing and appreciating everything. I was so filled with love, joy and peace. A peace that slowly started fading as anxiety and fear started slipping in as I thought of the next phase of my journey. Alice and I talked while I was away, and our desires to go in different directions was becoming very obvious. Her cruelty was increasing, or maybe my tolerance level was decreasing. Either way, there was obvious friction. I still had 3 weeks until my mom was flying in. I also had created some workshops and scheduled some events with Lis at Crossroads Gifts and Wellness. I had contract work scheduled that I committed to oversee and Alice and Ralph were going to take a vacation while I was there and could care for their cats. It was all set up, however, Alice changed while I was away building her bench. She spent a lot of time at Susun's, and each time we talked, there was more distance between us.

The closer it came to returning to their home, the weaker I became. The time away gave me an opportunity to really reflect on my time with Susun, running to Alice's and my experience with Alice.

While at Susun's I was getting up at 6am to go to AA meetings before rushing back to milk goats, and do the work I had agreed to. I shared this with Susun. I was very honest that I was going to meetings and really struggling. I had no desire to drink, I had a desire to be around acceptance, love, and support. Alice and I talked almost daily throughout this time. She talked me into coming to her home, assuring me it would be a safe place to really figure out what was going on. She also was excited to hire me to work with her brother, an addict.

Alice worked for Susun and went there regularly. As things unfolded after I left, Alice admitted to me she had been keeping secrets. She told me Susun had found a flask of vodka and I was being accused of drinking and hiding alcohol. Everything was starting to make sense. Susun told me she found vodka and asked me if I had some. I was very open that yes, I absolutely brought a gallon of vodka, along with jars, scissors and labels. I was using it to make tinctures. She informed me she had confiscated it. She was not comfortable with me having vodka, being in recovery and admitting I was going to meetings. I had nothing to hide and completely understood and respected her point. It was her home and I honored her decision. The thing that didn't make sense was that when I looked in my room, the gallon of vodka was still there. In my mind, if she was actually worried about me, then why would she leave the loaded gun in my room? I figured her contradiction was another test. Susun made it clear the first time around, she would contradict herself and purposely confuse us to make us find our center. She did so many things to force us to trust ourselves. I was no longer sure what was a test and what went too far. At the time I was in so deep, nothing made sense anymore. After hearing Alice's confession, I now realized that Susun believed the flask to be mine also. If this were true, it makes perfect sense why she would not trust me. No one uses a flask to make tinctures! We buy 100 proof vodka by the gallon to extract the plant medicine. Carrying a flask would make no sense when the goal is to tincture.

During the month at Alice's, it became clear. Alice knew about the flask, and about the gallon of vodka I had. She had all the pieces. I talked to her the night that Susun confronted me and shared with her how upset I was that Susun left it in my room. We were both unsure if it was a test or what was happening.

When Susun found out I was staying with Alice, it caused friction. After I first arrived at her house and Alice finally told me the truth about the flask, she was excited to see if she could help clear things up. She had all the pieces and wanted to tell Susun the truth. She knew I wasn't drinking, had no intention of drinking and really went out of my way to honor Susun. We were both hopeful to be able to clear the air.

I was in an extremely exhausted and vulnerable place when I finally made it to Alice's house. My entire world was being turned upside down. I needed time to really process everything I had just experienced and figure out what was real.

Alice and I talked daily about our experiences and really sifted through the transition. Learning that she had the power to clear up a huge misunderstanding was priceless. The realization that much of Susun's rage toward me was because she believed I was lying and drinking was heartbreaking to me. I loved and cherished all this woman taught me and the thought of her believing I betrayed her made me sick. I was so grateful Alice knew the truth and was going to help Susun and I heal our relationship.

Over the next few weeks, Alice continued her regular weekend visits to Susun's. The first weekend she returned saying she stuck up for me to the women who were there, not Susun. All the women were new and none had actually met me. I know from experience, there is a lot of energy and chaos when new apprentices arrive, especially four. It was no surprise when Alice shared there was an event that escalated, resulting in a woman being kicked. Alice explained that this was why she chose not to tell Susun the truth. She did however promise she would talk

to Susun and clear my name. She was very open about the fact
that she was scared and intimidated by Susun. She expressed
that Susun had talked about how strong I am. Alice told me
how strong I am. She was honest that she didn't feel as strong
or comfortable standing in her power. She never had, and did
not feel she could, confront Susun. She was terrified to tell
Susun that the flask wasn't mine and the more time passed, the
more fearful she became. She knew Susun would not believe
me or speak to me. She had the power the entire time to bring
clarity to Susun. Having all the pieces of the puzzle and the
power changed Alice.

I began to witness her behavior and listen to her words in an
observatory way; the way Susun taught me to assess situations.
What I learned was how Alice fed off the negative energy.
She loved having the power and loved going to Susun's when
there were new apprentices there. Alice shined and came alive
when the girls were crying and reaching out to her. She was
there for me when I was in pain. She loved being supportive.
When I stood in my power, talked about love, light, and moving
toward kindness, she shrank. I was learning her pattern. Her
words no longer affected me; it was her pattern that showed
me so much more.

As time passed, Alice would return from Susun's angrier and
angrier with both me and life. She never did tell Susun the
truth. Instead she fed off the anger and brought it home with
her. Ralph, other's living in the house, and I grew concerned. We
talked about an intervention or how we could help her. It was
obvious to everyone except Alice that her anger, aggressiveness
and abusiveness was amplified every time she returned. When
Susun called or left her messages, she was scared to answer the
phone. Instead she would tell stories of her misery and hatred
for Susun. She was terrified. Terrified of Susun, to stick up for
herself, her power, and to break the cycle. There was definitely
a duality and she did not want to see it.

When Alice invited me in, she also contracted me to do
energy work on her. I did a few sessions. One of the things she
really wanted to work on was her relationship trauma with her

mom. Since I met her, she had told me how toxic their relationship was. She explained how her mom created this illusion of love and opportunity. She would hire people, invite them in and after the work was done, find fault, hate them, blame them and then never pay them what was earned. Instead she would be extremely cruel until they just left and didn't care about getting paid. She shared that her mom invited me to work there, but she was protecting me from the cruelty and would not allow me to meet her mother. She intentionally built a wall, never wanting us to meet. Alice didn't want her mom to drive a wedge between us like she did her childhood friend. Alice carried much hatred and blame toward her mother for the loss of this friend. She explained to me how her friend was so psychic that she could hear Alice's mom every time they were together. She had to break ties and couldn't have Alice in her life anymore. Alice blamed her mom for many things, no friends being the biggest one.

It all made sense to me. I could see everything. When Alice and I were working together, I asked her if she wanted to know what I saw. I asked her if she wanted help with the anger, blame, and to possibly heal the relationship with her friend. She declined. She said she wanted to stay in the dark and wasn't willing to see what I saw. She wasn't ready. She was attached to the story and closed to anything that threatened it. I knew this behavior well, I was once attached to many stories and labels, bipolar, ADHD, eating disorder, depression, etc. Labels become our identity. Stories keep us sick. I also knew that I could not help her, she had to want to see. If I pushed, it would only ignite a defense that made her sink deeper into her story and hold on tighter. I had to just love her and walk away.

Things shifted quickly. She opened the door for me to help her and then got scared. The more she knew I could see, the angrier she got. She no longer wanted to pay me for my services and said she had no intention of clearing my name with Susun. She said it was my problem. She extended the offer to still house sit for her and the cats, meet with the contractors and finish what I started so she could go on vacation. She followed that invitation with I want you out of my house and my sight when I return. She offered a fraction of the money she had committed to, thinking I would take the offer because I was stuck and needed to actually get paid by her. She used it all as leverage.

Alice knew that I had to stay in the area, that my mom bought a plane ticket to meet me based on the timing Alice asked for and the workshops I scheduled. Alice was the one who contracted my services and encouraged me to make all the other plans. She was so excited about the ceremonial work we did, along with all the things I had done for her both spiritually and around her house. She asked for more. That is, until it came time to pay! The closer I got to returning and delivering her bench, the meaner she became.

Everything was so clear to me. I had no idea what I was going to do, but I knew I couldn't go back there. I had scheduled workshops with Lis at Crossroads Gifts and Wellness. My mom wasn't flying in for another three weeks and couldn't change her timeline. I had barely any money left since Alice decided not to pay and I had no idea where I was going to stay. I was at a loss.

I did what I would tell a client to do, what I had trained myself to do. I asked the universe to show me, guide me, help me see what the best path for me was. Then I get quiet. I walked. I sat. I allowed the message to come to me. Lis. You have to be willing to be vulnerable, honest, humble and ask for help. Call Lis.

I was terrified of this message. I had just met Lis, she wanted to help promote my business, my expertise, my book, my success. How could I possibly call her and ask for help? If I let her see my fear, my weakness, my vulnerability, she may see me as drama and not want anything to do with me. All the worst-case scenarios came to my mind. I was so scared to ask Lis for help, to let her see me, really see me.

I also knew that if the universe is guiding me, then I need to listen. It does no good to ask for help and then ignore the guidance. I teach people, ask and then trust. Trust what doesn't make sense. The fear is an illusion to keep you stuck. Run toward what scares you the most. What scares you the most is your path to true freedom and liberation. I knew it, I teach it, I have supported so many clients along this path. Yet doing it alone was so scary. I had taken these leaps before, and every time they worked out.

Have you ever been in one of these crossroads? You know the right thing to do, yet you are still terrified? You feel backed in a corner and your options are to stay stuck in the pain or to move through the fear and be open to the possibility of relief? It's amazing how hard it is no matter how many times you have been there before.

I called Lis. I asked if I could stay with her. I shared with her that I was in a transitional period and was confused. I was honest. I was terrified of rejection and judgement. I opened up and was completely exposed. I allowed myself to be vulnerable.

Lis opened her heart and her home to me. Lis showed me it was safe to be vulnerable. Lis invited me in and showed me the light. She wanted to help me. This was completely opposite of what I had experienced in the past. Lis transformed my belief about showing my weakness.

When I was living in the dark, showing my weakness opened the door to be controlled. My previous experiences taught me that allowing people to know I was hurting and scared opened me up to more pain. I had experienced my vulnerability being used against me, as leverage. I had a huge fear of asking for help. Especially after what I just went through with Alice and Susun. I trusted them and now here I am opening up to a complete stranger. This stranger, Lis, showed me more kindness than the women who were supposed to have had my back. Lis showed me the way people that Love themselves and teach with compassion act. She showed me a different way. And this was just the beginning of what this angel modeled for me.

I wrestled with the idea of reaching out to Susun, clearing my name myself. The anger and betrayal I felt was so painful. I wanted to expose Alice. Susun teaches women to take responsibility for themselves. She also has a powerful network of allies that fought for women's rights and have each other's backs. I knew that if she was aware that Alice knew the truth about the flask this entire time, she would never look at Alice the same. Susun hates weakness and I can only imagine how disgusted she would be to know that Alice could have shared the truth but chose to hide it. I wanted Alice to feel the pain and betrayal I felt. I wanted Susun to see the truth about her.

I wrote several letters to Susun. I burned every one. I never reached out to Susun. I chose to let it all go. Hurt people hurt people. Had I exposed Alice at that time, it would have been me seeking revenge. Revenge only lowers me to her level. I chose to move toward love, light and taking the high road. Alice was her mother and she hated me for seeing it. She had no friends. Everything about her reminded me of how I acted when I hated myself. Hurting her would have just been cruel, she was already dead inside. Running to Susun and defending my honor only made me look and feel weak. I had nothing to prove. I did nothing wrong. Lis helped me with this decision. I had to get the trauma out of me. It was in my cells, consuming my mind and making me sick. Lis helped me work through the pain both physically and emotionally. I wrote letters and burned them until my hand hurt. Lis did energy work on me helping clear and heal. I don't know what I would have done without her.

Reflections

I remembered being scared of my power and feeding off others pain. My actions came from a place of fear. I connected with others through pain, it was all I knew. Helping them distracted me from feeling my own. It wasn't until the fear of the unknown hurt less than the pain of staying that I broke the cycle.

I had to first acknowledge the cycle to break it.

I had to choose to look backwards, clear my name, seek revenge, and continue to fight

Or

I had to surrender and be open to a softer, gentler, more loving way. I was being given the opportunity to consciously see where I came from and choose to truly honor where I claimed I wanted to go.

I chose to let go of everything I knew, everything I experienced, all the stories attached to what was happening and focus on where I wanted to go.

I was done fighting. I was ready for love.

Opportunities

What stories are you holding onto?

What patterns are you afraid to see or break?

What thoughts make you feel weak and sick?

Write them all down. Write letters to anyone you are carrying anger toward. Write out all the pain and rage you want to scream about.

Then burn them! Ask that the universe transmute all that pain into love and refill you.

This is the best way to release yourself from suffering without hurting anyone else, fighting, or making yourself vulnerable. You burn it so no one else can read it and you never want to reread it. The point is to let it go. To read it only puts it back in. BURN IT!

CHOOSING THE LIGHT

August

The universe was absolutely fulfilling my intention to experience life on a scale bigger than my mind could comprehend and aligning me with people, places and experiences that support my stepping into the love and light! I was able to seamlessly transition from Tupper Lake to Schenectady, where I was gifted more opportunities that I would not have known how to ask for. Choosing to move through my fear and embrace vulnerability seemed to be getting easier. The more I chose to surrender, the more evidence I received that my prayers were being answered.

Not only did Lis and I pull of an amazing workshop at her home that transformed all the participants, but she also promoted my services in her store, Crossroads Gifts and Wellness. I was blessed to do several healing sessions, Intuitive readings and connect to some absolutely genuine people that captivated me.

I was invited to be part of a Global Peace Project. Mary Clare, one of Lis's friends invited me to share a meditation for the project at her Studio, Yoga Bliss. I was able to join her and many others to record guided meditations to support the cause. Global Peace Project is an annual event to raise the consciousness, awareness and vibration of the community. What an honor and a blessing it was for me to have the privilege of both witnessing and participating in such a special event. I had the opportunity to meet some phenomenal people and learn so many ways to share, support and spread light and love.

The magic seemed to be expanding, my intentions were working. I was manifesting everything I wanted. One of the things I was learning about manifesting and changing my reality was that feeling what I wanted to experience while visualizing it is what helps both me and the universe get crystal clear on what I am calling in. I had 2 weeks left with Lis. I utilized the time I had left to focus, feel and project as much clarity as possible.

I was happy. Everything was falling into place seamlessly, as requested!

All I could think about was how excited I was to meet back up with Henry and go to Costa Rica. I really believed that this was finally my time; my time to fall in love and finally move through life with a partner. When I thought of this, the realization came back that I had not experienced a healthy relationship. I needed to explore what healthy meant to me. I needed to explore what I wanted to experience. What did I envision for an emotionally healthy relationship? What would happiness feel like in my mind and body? What does making love feel like? Or what do I want to feel? I had never really thought about this before.

I sat down and really asked myself these questions... Originally, I wrote my intentions specifically about what I wanted to experience with Henry. Then I was guided to make them about what I wanted to experience, period. If Henry was the man for me, we would align beautifully. If he was not, I will be calling in the man of my dreams. So, I wrote out my new intentions of meeting my dream partner.

I intend I see my path unfolding easily and effortlessly in front of me. I intend I always know the best next move quickly and intuitively responding with grace and ease. I intend I am a lighthouse, a source of power, with love and integrity. I intend I am in perfect union with my higher self and the universe as spirit works through me. I intend my medicine is sought after, recognized and respected. I intend I am compensated generously, easily, and effortlessly. I AM TRUTH. Truth sets people free. I AM LOVE. Love opens hearts and restores hope, faith, and Trust. I am clairvoyant and clairaudient. I intend to have all resources I need, they come to me easily and effortlessly in abundance, with plenty to use, plenty to spare, and plenty to share. I intend all resources show up easily and effortlessly in abundance before they are necessary. I intend I align with the perfect property to share my gifts, be steward of the land and live in harmony as it comes to me easily and effortlessly. I intend I live a life filled with joy, laughter, love and abundance. I intend I align with my male partner seamlessly and effortlessly, with love, joy, abundance, passion, and grace. I see him with blue eyes, well-traveled, secure, confident and great with money. He is flexible, compassionate, wise, and we can learn from each other. I asked to be magnetically drawn to him.

I intend to get swept up in LOVE and bring out the best of myself and others, with love, honor, compassion and support. I intend I live harmoniously, and always have the means, power, clarity, and willingness to expand, travel, and grow, creating a life more abundant and magical than I could comprehend at this time. I intend I am honored; my body, mind, spirit, soul, and my medicine. I intend to be seen and heard, laugh often, and allow my inner child to play. I intend to see both light and dark with clarity. I intend I see both light and dark with compassion and grace. I intend my life be filled with experiences, people, opportunities, love, laughter and abundance on a scale bigger than I could possibly comprehend in this moment. I intend I am guarded, guided and protected at all times. I AM Happy, Healthy and Whole. I intend all is for the highest and greatest good of everyone, everywhere, the universe and myself. So mote it be.

I needed to know what this actually felt like in my body. I wanted to empower and magnify my intentions and I knew how. Every morning for the next 2 weeks, I did ceremonial work and focused all my energy on getting crystal clear on what I wanted to experience.

I lit a candle, then I lit incense, with the intention that the candle open up the space for my dreams to come true and the incense surround and protect them. After reading the intentions out loud, I went and meditated. I asked myself the questions again. What do I want to feel? What is healthy sex? What does that feel like in my body? What does my body like? How does my body want to be touched? What turns me on?

I actually went out in nature, got quiet, got comfortable and explored these questions. I slowly undressed myself, just like I wanted to be undressed. I rubbed my feet. I rubbed my legs. I explored all the foreplay I wanted to experience. I caressed my entire body, slowly. I touched myself everywhere, really seeing what my body both felt like to me and what it felt like to be touched gently. I touched my face, my neck, my breasts and continued down my stomach. I explored my nipple sensation, my lips, my everything. I explored my vagina, what felt good, what didn't. I got comfortable feeling myself, understanding the pressure I liked, understanding when and how I enjoy penetration, teasing etc. I got really clear on my body and what feels good to me. I then visualized and felt the energy of a man touching me. I had learned to imagine the energy I want to experience vs a specific man. I imagined an energy that honored my desires, my boundaries, my body. I imagined a man that was secure and confident in himself. I imagined a man so in love with me that he was willing to go slow, allowing me to be comfortable. I imagined that he was understanding that this was new to me and wanted to explore every inch of my body with me. He wanted to know what turned me on and what was better left alone. He wanted to please me, knowing that it would also please him. I imagined the man that I just connected with. I felt the man that was also seeking a mutually loving, honoring, healthy relationship. I felt the man that resonated with my core frequencies. I felt our love and passion come together easily and effortlessly as we were magnetically drawn together. I saw us traveling, exploring the world, exploring each other, laughing, and loving each other. I felt us honoring, respecting and inspiring each other. I felt us bringing out the best in one another and having each other's back, no matter what. I felt us living in the highest light, serving with love and living the dream. I felt the win/win/win I was seeking.

I did this ceremony daily for 2 weeks. I was committed. And then I let it all go and trusted.

Meanwhile...

Lis and I really bonded and did some deep healing work together. I learned so much about this amazing woman. She is a true medicine woman and healer. She has so many gifts. Her energy, her insight, her ability to see was incredible to witness. I watched the way she was with people. The way they reacted to her. She was humble, vulnerable, honest and so real. Lis was the example I wanted to rise up to. She offered support, community, teachings, and helped people with kindness, compassion and love. I learned so much from her. She was my angel; she is many people's angel.

I met Myron, this magical author I was blessed to spend time with. He did a session with me. The session opened up a duality that he was willing to discuss live. We explored the contrast between light and darkness, how to utilize it and then alchemize it! You can find the replay rewritingyourreality.com.

I was also blessed to meet a unique soul named Gary. Gary introduced me to his world of magic, vulnerability and beauty. He trusted me and opened up. He allowed me to see him, all of him.

Both of these men trusted me fully. They allowed me in their energy, to see everything. The healing that came from the experience was beyond what any of us expected. Both of these men have incredible gifts and I feel special to have been the woman they trusted to hold space as they unlocked and released more layers. They are lighthouses.

I also found another group of people that I cannot mention by name, however spending time with them impacted my life. It was the most magical secret society. A secret society that is everywhere and anyone desiring to free themselves from the bondage of poison is welcome. The people I met there aligned with everything I had been seeking; family, community, love. This group of people, welcomed me, embraced me, accepted me, and showed me so much about their culture. They were raw. They were real. They said it how it was, no BS, no sugar, just straight up honesty. They had each other's backs. They gave community support a whole new meaning for me. To all those amazing people, the family from the Schenectady Clubhouse, thank you. It was an honor to be a guest and a speaker. I appreciate you. Keep coming back.

Reflections

Choosing to cut my losses, ask for help and trust the universe was the best decision I could have made. I could feel a shift in my body. The sickness I felt from my experiences with Susun and Alice were gone. I felt energized, alive, alert and full of creative flow. I was connected to my body. I was listening to everything I felt. Yes, listening to the feeling. Amplifying my awareness of what feels good and what doesn't. Honoring every move with clarity and conscious choices.

My relationship with my inner compass was stronger than ever as I flowed from one experience to the next. Letting go of resistance, expectation, resentments, the fight, the need to prove, old beliefs, old patterns, old ideas...

Opportunities

What experience do you want to create?

How does it feel in your body?

Who do you want to share it with? The energy of the person, not specific people.

Write out exactly what you want to experience, feel, see, hear. Use all your senses.

Then visualize it, feel it, experience it in your mind. What are you wearing, what time of day is it, what's the temperature, really live it in your mind.

NEW PERSPECTIVES

August

Is there anyone in your life that you have a love/hate relationship with?

Possibly codependent or confusing? You know they love you, however the interaction leaves you feeling powerless and drained?

This was my mom and me.

I picked her up at the Albany, NY airport and we were on our way to Niagara Falls, through Canada to Michigan. I had not been back to Michigan since I got sober. For me, it always felt good to see my mom. She has been my biggest supporter, my biggest fan and been there for me every step of the way. However, it didn't take long before our excitement turned into fighting and tears. When we were together, it felt like she was talking to the 15-year-old version of me rather than the strong, independent, competent woman standing before her.

It was like she created opportunities to save me or help me. Her actions came from a place of helpful intent, however they actually created pain and chaos for me. It was difficult for her to just be and allow me to just be. It was a cycle and I could see it clearly. I understood it. The version of me she was talking to didn't exist anymore and she wasn't coming back! I let go of that and was ready to help her let go too. This was our cycle and it was about to break!

My mom carried a lot of guilt over my past. She had one goal, to love and protect me. There is no question that every decision she made came from a place of love and what she believed to be the best for me. To have an alcoholic daughter with an eating disorder that seemed to go from one abusive relationship to the next took a toll on her and our relationship. She couldn't protect me and she somehow blamed herself. She was still carrying all the pain of witnessing and somewhat enabling my chaotic past. I had let go and changed who I am. That version of me died a few years ago and I was not about to allow this cycle to resurface. I now had one goal, help her let go of everything, just like I had. She was willing.

I pulled the car over and we went into nature. She was open and I shared with her a new way to see, a new way to be and a new way to let go. She wanted to understand and wanted to let go. We talked, we cried, we released, and we grounded that energy down. It was life altering. Out of respect for my mom's privacy, I will not go into more detail. What I can share is that our relationship since that day has never been better. We left so much behind, emerging as strong women who see each other. We honor each other and have each other's backs. We are allies. We communicate in an entirely new way. I am crying while I am typing this for how blessed I feel. I know I am so lucky my mom was willing and open to doing the work with me. Together we have supported each other through some painful and intense experiences. We completely shifted our entire reality because we loved each other enough to look at ourselves and do whatever it took to fully show up for ourselves first, and then for one another.

Our new way of being and seeing each other allowed us to really create some new memories. I had done so much personal growth. In my shamanic training, I was taught to see multiple perspectives, views, angles, and ideas. I had been training myself and practicing this for a few years. To be able to share what I see and help her see was amazing. She was so open and willing, although with a lot of skepticism! It takes time to see certain things. The illusions, the patterns, the worlds, the shadows; it can be very overwhelming. It can also be very painful when we gain a full understanding of what we are actually witnessing. The awareness takes time to integrate.

Niagara Falls was a fabulous opportunity to practice this integration and really enjoy our new relationship before getting to my brother's. It was pretty cool when my mom was able to experience him differently too. She was seeing everything with all her love and a new perspective. It was beautiful to witness.

Michigan was extremely healing for me, sober for the first time, experiencing people and places that once intimidated me. To be able to face my home town, a place I had only know when I was extremely sick and addicted, was so healing. I released so much pain, fear, anxiety and judgement. Judgment of both myself and others. Judgement of my past. Shame. Blame. Guilt. I let it all go. I left with an entirely new perspective on my past, myself and my future. No more hiding. Head high, confident and proud. I know my power.

As mom and I headed south, we had only one more stop before Florida. Indianapolis, to see Lori. Ironically, Lori is a friend from high school that I don't think I had seen since graduation. It had been 20 years! She is another angel. Lori and I reconnected after I finished my first book, *I'm Sober, Now What? Moving though the fear, anxiety and humility of LIFE, on Life's terms*. She has been one of the few people I have reconnected with that fully supports my sobriety. I had reached out to many of the people I thought were my friends. Most will have nothing to do with me. Recovery is an interesting, rewarding and painful journey. The hardest thing for me was to realize that my 'friends' were not really friends, and never were. They were people who reflected where I was at the time, I was sick. We spent time together, because we accepted, tolerated and fed each other's addictions. The second I raised my standards, the relationships all changed. My getting better threatened their way of being. Behavior I once tolerated and participated in was no longer acceptable to me. As I began to love myself, those who were not ready to see the new me shut me out. The more I changed, the more I saw. It was painful being on the other side of cruelty I once engaged in. It sucked, yet was also very healing. I was able to see how I acted and how my actions were received by others. The experience allowed me to have compassion for everyone involved. I thank Susun for training me to face life and stand in my power. And I thank friends like Lori, who opened her home, her heart and her world to me. She has gone out of her way to support my growth and been an amazing friend. I was so excited to see her.

I learned so much form my visit with Lori. We pulled out all her photo albums from High School and reminisced about the past. Lori shared with me her perspectives and how she remembered events. It was fascinating to really understand how we each experienced the same events so drastically different. I loved seeing through her eyes, hearing her version of history, or in this case, her-story. Her energy, her views, her acceptance and openness were a breath of fresh air. I appreciate her so much and am so grateful to have her in my life today.

Lori showed me acceptance. We have known each other since fifth grade. When I reached out to her, she was so open and inviting. All she wanted to do was help me. She wanted to understand me, she cared about my journey, she saw how much I struggled. She witnessed my pain and fed my growth. She never judged, she shared with me her perspective. She helped me make sense of what I went through. She offered me answers and shed light into my blind spots with compassion and kindness. She loved me and wanted to help me be the best version of me. She celebrates my ability to move through the pain and turn it into something useful. She's a gift.

Reflections

Peer pressure can be heavy, painful, exhausting. To change a cycle requires perseverance; it is not easy, however, it is rewarding. To anyone making a shift, keep going. Once you move through the initial break from the pact, more support than you imagined will show up. Trust that you are supported. Support will come when you least expect it in ways you couldn't predict.

My mom was willing to make the shift with me. She had invested in and supported me for years. It would have been so easy for me to live my new life and alienate her. I have met many people who have transformed and walked away to support their own healing. I get it. There is a fine line between enabling and support. My mom and I worked through all of this together. There is no question that I am fortunate that my mom was willing to look at the patterns and create change with me. If the person you love/hate is willing to discover new patterns with you and support your change, I encourage you to take the time to relearn together. To be able to heal together and break family cycles is priceless.

The patterns and the roles we adopt are so powerful. What protected us as a child, destroys us as adults. The body armor becomes thick and unconscious.

Opportunities

Write down people and places where you feel powerless or intimidated.

Pick one. See yourself as a character, how does your character play the same role every time? Identify the pattern.

How can you change the pattern or role to empower yourself?

Write out a new scenario, one that empowers every character.

Look at your new pattern, put yourself in another person's role. As this person, do you still feel empowered?

If you do, congratulations! Try it out next time.

If not, how can you create an opportunity where you feel empowered and respected playing each role?

This may take a few times to work through. If there is someone you trust that would be willing to role play or offer another perspective, ask them.

If you don't have anyone you trust, schedule a discovery call with me and let's talk it out!

THE HUSTLE

September

Henry was special to me. We met over three years ago when I was very fresh in my sobriety. I hadn't dated sober before. I hadn't been with a man sober. I waited over a year to start dating, as suggested, to really get to know myself before opening that door. All I knew was toxic. The last man I was with was the reason I chose to get sober. I wanted to put a gun to his head so he couldn't hurt anyone else and then put the gun to my own to make the pain stop. So when I met Henry, I was vulnerable, scared, and very new to the dating world. He was patient. He was kind. He honored my boundaries and was willing to go as slow as I needed. We never really discussed outcomes or the future, we just saw each other when we saw each other, which was often.

After about six months, we started getting intimate. He was the first man I allowed to get that close to me, it was terrifying. I felt so awkward and uncomfortable; however, he was gentle, kind, and put me at ease. I felt like he really cared for me.

Soon after, he informed me that he was seeing another woman as well. Around that same time, I had opened up to someone from my past as well. I reunited with someone that claimed to really love me and wanted to try us again now that I was sober. I needed to know if my drinking was the problem or the relationship just wasn't right, so I was open to exploring who I was and what I really wanted. Henry and I went our separate ways.

A few months went by and I heard from Henry again. We were both single again. He invited me over and we started spending a lot of time together again. We got along great and it felt like we could have a future together. There were a lot of red flags though. I was still learning my boundaries, who I was and how to be, sober. I was finding my way. While I believed he wanted to help me and cared about me, there were things that just didn't feel right. Little things like the way he touched me, the way he talked to me. I couldn't quite put my finger on what it was, but I knew something wasn't right. I often left feeling dirty and drained.

Henry is a hustler, and a damn good one at that. Over the years, I learned so much from him. He explained to me that he sees every situation as a win/lose and he will win no matter what. At first this didn't make sense to me. I thought he was referring to business deals and how to negotiate. I listened. I watched. I studied how he interacted with people, the words he used. I learned how he played on people's emotions and took advantage of every situation he could. His door was always open; he calls his house the house of abundance. People were always welcome. They would come and party, hang out, socialize, etc. He was always hosting, making food, treating everyone like family. I thought he really cared about all these people. I thought they were his friends. I met some really great people. I also thought I was special and he really cared about me. He seemed to support my business, I even brought clients to his house and did sessions there when I needed a private room. His support felt amazing, yet there was still something off.

Over time, it started to make sense. I was seeing clearer and clearer. I was growing, evolving and seeing that some of the help, wasn't actually help. The stronger, healthier and more comfortable I got in my skin and in my boundaries, the more distant Henry got. It was silly things, too. He wanted me at his house, knew the one thing that would make me happy was a hammock. I had two things that I loved, my morning yoga and laying in a hammock. I loved to read, relax, etc. I did not need much. He told me for three years that he had a hammock in his attic. For three years he said he would put it out for me.

Another big red flag was emotions. When he had a prostate scare, he leaned on me hard. I was there. When I would cry, he got uncomfortable and was mean. He didn't know how to handle my emotions or didn't care too. I actually tried to teach him, I explained that when I am crying, all I need is you to put your arms around me and hug me. Holding me is the best gift you can give to me; I just want to be able to fall into your arms and know you are there. He looked at me like he saw a ghost.

It wasn't long after that I walked away. I wanted someone who wanted me. I wanted to experience love with someone who was able to handle my emotions and wanted to be there for me. I wanted a mutually beneficial experience.

This was the second time I had walked away from Henry. I was done. He was and always would be special to me, however, I wanted more. I made that clear.

So when he reached out months later, told me his life was better with me in it and offered to fly anywhere to see me, I was excited. I thought maybe he was ready to step up. I was open to the possibility that this man actually did some work and wanted me in his life. I was clear. I was honest about what I wanted out of a relationship, what I was pursuing on my adventure and where I wanted to go. When I asked him to please respect my choices and to be honest, I believed he was. I asked him to let me go if he did not see himself with me. I was so open, vulnerable and honest. He still flew up to see me and wanted to go to Costa Rica. He was sure that the retreat center in Costa Rica was perfect for what I wanted to build. I had every reason and every faith to believe that we were moving toward a future. Not only had he still wanted to go on the trip, but he was also open to participating in the work I do. He had witnessed transformations people had after energy sessions with me, yet never allowed me to work on him. He was never open to it in his home since his doors were always open. He made it clear that if he were going experience my kind of work, it could not be near where we lived. He shared that he was open to the work and the healing. His commitment was the tipping point that convinced me to agree to the trip. He had been terrified of the thought of surrendering control and letting go. When he said he trusted me, wanted me in his life and was open to it, I agreed instantly. I was so excited.

In my mind, I thought our trip, two weeks together was our opportunity to reconnect, let go of the past and see how we were without any distractions. I thought it would be romantic and fun. I was so excited to be alone with a man that was so special to me and see what the future held. He planned for us to go a few different places before heading to the Valley where the retreat center was. I was open to the journey. All I cared about was spending time with him and seeing where it went. He had sent me pictures of the places he chose, with hammocks, bikes, close to the beach. I thought he really got me and wanted to show me he had changed. Man was I wrong!

His friend picked us up after a couple days to head to another beach before going to the valley. I learned so much. Nothing had changed. My feelings, emotions, and anything below the surface was still unacceptable. All I did with my vulnerability was teach Henry how to manipulate me better. It didn't take me long to realize what was happening. He always wins. I was a game. I felt sick.

I didn't even see it at first, I was too blinded by hope and giving him the benefit of the doubt. His friend and some other men that did some spiritual work with me helped me see. They modeled how men who actually have your best interest at heart act. They were willing to talk about emotions and things that are real. They were kind and loving to me, in a healthy, respectful way. I had some long conversations with a spiritual healer who really helped me see that I deserve better and that there are so many men out there that respect, honor and cherish women. He helped me understand how the play on words was being used and pointed me in a direction to learn more. I was grateful.

I knew by going to Costa Rica that Henry and I would either live happily ever after or never speak again. I really was hopeful for the first one. On the way home, he didn't even stand in line with me at the airport, he had a global entry pass, I didn't. He left me to stand in one line while he fast tracked. He didn't care about me. There was no team, no love, just how can he serve himself.

When we got back to Florida, he actually invited me to go away for the weekend with him again, this time to a festival. It was a music festival that you dress up for and it really looked fun. He knew my buttons, he showed me one of the stages, it was surrounded by hammocks! He was sure I would love it and insisted he wanted me there as life is more fun with me there. I laughed. I was low on cash after all my travels and though the festival looked fun, I really didn't want to spend time with Henry. There was a group going and I opened up to the idea for a minute. Henry told me the cost and said go earn some money and come, I want you there. I had a bunch of art that I was trying to sell. He made some calls offering to help me sell some. As he looked through it, there were two pieces he really liked. I told him he could have them. I appreciated that he was trying to help me sell them. He hung them on his wall, and then said, "now go earn some money so you can come to the festival." That was the day. This man laughs about spending $40,000 cash for a new vehicle and loans people $100,000's cash. He was happy to take my art and offer nothing and then tell me to go earn so I can be with him. I was entertainment. I wanted to vomit. It's easy to be abundant when you surround yourself with givers and feed off them. Or in my case, the perfect victim. I was still in needy mode in the love department!

I told him we could never be; I will always lose since I only seek win/win. He looked confused. I thanked him. I now understand the game, I learned the lesson and will never subject myself to men like him again.

What an incredibly painful gift. Henry taught me so much about a world I had no idea about. I learned how to spot the hustle, the quick talking mind games, and ways I was vulnerable. He exposed my people pleasing and how I gave my power away. I learned to observe, feel, and trust myself over the illusion. I taught him how to control me by telling him what was important to me. He was a master at tapping into my feelings.

I always looked for the win/win. I would self-sacrifice before taking from someone else, to a fault. That fault was the needy/victim energy I was still carrying. I was able to see where I could love myself more and how to put my needs first. I was able to see where I could have used my voice and asked him to buy my art and support me. There were so many opportunities for personal growth, loving him blinded me. Letting go and loving myself allowed me to practice healthier boundaries, and see how I was allowing myself to be controlled by my emotions. Powerful clarity for me. What a priceless gift.

Reflections

I had to fall in love with myself to see the truth. I learned to separate from my emotions to see the bigger picture. I had to be willing to stop lying to myself and let go of my expectations or how I thought it would look. I had to face my neediness and figure out how I can make better use of that energy. Love myself more?

This took looking at why I allowed him to be more important than my voice, my needs, my well-being. It hurt!

Always remember, people are teaching you everything you need to know by how they treat themselves, how the treat others and how they speak about things. Likewise, you are teaching people about you. You teach them how to treat you by how you treat yourself, what you accept and what you allow.

Opportunities

Make a list of the people you feel you need, for any reason.

Write down what you think the need is.

Go through and ask yourself, can I live without that?

If yes, great! How does knowing you don't need them change the way you feel?

If the answer is no, you can't live without it, can you do it for yourself?

If no, keep going. Who else could possibly help you? Where else can I get this information? Where can I learn? Keep going until you no longer need that person.

How has your energy changed?

NEW CHOICES

October

Landmark Forum. This was the direction I was pointed to while in Costa Rica. I signed up. The majority of my training and the work I had done was shamanic. I work with different realms, energy, and nonphysical reality. I have had much success and was now being guided to go deeper. One of the reoccurring messages I had been receiving was truth. Words and truth. I know our words create our reality and that by changing our words, we can completely alter our reality. I had done it, witnessed it and lived it. I saw this as an opportunity to take it to another level. I am always excited to invest in myself and learn as much as possible.

It reminded me of story medicine, something I used often with clients and it is a powerful tool. I learned about story medicine during my shamanic training. We give experiences power through the story we attach to it. We have the choice to tell the story however we wish. There are so many perspectives. The story can free us, trap us, label us or delete us. The identity or voice we choose shapes our reality. There's the hero, the victim, the martyr, the child, the spectator, and so many more. Are you aware of the view you tell your stories from?

The experience was life altering. I learned a new language. I learned a new way to express what I had been doing, along with more self-discovery. I was so impressed and excited that I signed up for the next course and went on another three-month journey through the advanced course. The experience was equally eye opening. I am like a sponge and love learning new ways to accomplish the same experience. I was able to integrate all the new ways of communicating into my practice. The more languages I learn the more people I can communicate with. This new language allows me to work with people in worlds that were foreign to me. I am able to connect to more people and broaden my ability to communicate with my clients. I learn through doing the work on myself first. The group was over 100 people and broke into smaller teams to do the actual weekly work and hold each other accountable. I was my group leader which allowed me to do have double the opportunity for meetings and growth. I met with the course leader and other leaders as well as holding my own group accountable. It was a wonderful experience. I love being both student and teacher, there are always opportunities to grow!

One of the ladies in our group was a mother whose daughters were also having a rough time. Her oldest daughter struggled with addiction. I was blessed with a very generous and loving team. I gifted her one of my books, *I'm Sober, Now What? Moving through the fear, anxiety and humility of LIFE, on Life's terms,* and myself and two other team members combined our resources and gifted her the first course, Landmark Forum. It was beautiful. Again, the universe was delivering what I asked for seamlessly. I was in a position to share and give back or pay it forward! I was working with a team of people who had each other's backs and helped each other. I knew I was still on the right path.

Everything seemed to be unfolding as seamlessly and effortlessly as indented, until it didn't.

During this time, Don's health was declining rapidly. The day came, the one when he couldn't get up. We knew it was no longer a matter of if, but when. After that day, he never got up again. He was in bed for the next few weeks.

To fully grasp the impact this had on my life, you need to understand Don's role in my growth. Don entered my life sixteen years prior; I was 27. I was still very deep in my dis-ease, a drunk and very sick. He married my mom and welcomed me into his heart and family, knowing I was in a state of emotional chaos. He loved me and helped me. He was there when I washed two bottles of pills down with vodka, and was confused as to how I woke up. He was there for the three months of rehab. He helped me apply for financial aid and go back to school after getting out. Don helped me figure out how to take my power back. He was so supportive to both my mom and me through my process of recovery, self-discovery and growth. He did everything he could to help me better myself. He showed me unconditional love. He modeled behavior that I needed to see.

This caused me to reflect on my inability to be there for my stepbrother, Kirk's death 8 years prior. I had the privilege of getting to know him very well. He invited me to start over and live with him in North Carolina. He was going through a divorce and needed help with his boys. I needed a new start. He opened his home, introduced me to his friends and gave me the space to grow. While I made some powerful shifts, like quitting smoking and was able to tutor and be there for his kids, I was still drinking. Even after rehab, I drank for nine more years. I was really trapped in the darkness of addiction. It's a horrible disease and I started spiraling out of control again. I did some really stupid things while I was drinking. One bad decision led to another, compounding the shame and guilt. Then I would drink more to not feel the toxic feelings, it was horrible. I eventually made a pretty big mistake that summer, one that couldn't be ignored. One of the neighbors caught wind of it and tried to blackmail me. Kirk blocked it. He had no reason to help me. I hid everything from him and put him in an uncomfortable and unfair position. He had my back anyway. In my experience, I learned that whether I own my behavior or just get caught, the consequences were the same and it's better to hide. He showed me that I could take responsibility. He taught me to stop hiding. He showed me forgiveness, understanding and acceptance. He showed me that we can disagree and he would still be there for me. Kirk taught me that as family, we support each other. He was the first man in my life to show me this kind of love and support. He didn't belittle me, he opened up an opportunity for me to rise to the occasion. He was the first man to see how sick, scared, lost and broken I was and show me love. I was used to being told repeatedly what was wrong with me and wanting to die. Kirk had every right to be angry with me and chose to love me anyway. He changed my life. Soon after, I moved back to Florida. He got cancer and passed. I was still very sick and not able to be there for him. That is something I have to live with.

So when Don got sick, there was no question where I wanted to be. He and Kirk showed me so much love and support, I was finally in a position to give back. I will never forget the day Don realized he wasn't getting up again. He had tears in his eyes and was saying how humiliated he felt. I started crying with gratitude, all I could say was "you were there for me when I was sick and this is your karma. You taught me how to love and now I get to love you and be there for you. Thank you for this honor." Don was so special to me and I could not think of anywhere I would rather be.

Reflections

I had to make the choice to go along my merry way or stay and help with Don's transition. The contrast of not being able to support Kirk and be present with him is something I have to live with. It's an awareness I carry. I was not going to have the same experience with Don. I now had the choice to choose a different path and be the person I wanted to be. I was willing to change my plans and commit to my family. We all had to surrender to Don's timeline and allow the experience to run its course. I had no control over how long this would take or how it played out. I could control me and I was honored to be there as he crossed. I was honored to be there for my mom and for my stepsister who was also very present along this journey.

I used to think I was being selfish; I didn't look at myself. I did what everyone else wanted and then was empty and resentful. That behavior led to destruction. That behavior was why I wasn't able to be there for Kirk. Choosing to be selfish, to own my choices and take responsibility for my life was actually the most selfless act I ever did. As I shifted into taking responsibility for my actions, my thoughts, my health, my attitude, I fell in love with myself. The more I loved myself, the easier it was to show up for others. The more I loved myself and took responsibility for myself, the less others had to worry about me. By being selfish and taking care of my needs, I was able to show up strong, filled, and ready to serve.

The most selfless act you can offer is to selfishly take care of yourself. You cannot fill another if your cup is empty.

These actions honored what Kirk taught me and allowed me to show up fully for Don.

When your cup is full, you can then be fully present with others and that is the best gift you can give.

Opportunities

Are you clear that you cannot help, save, or show up for anyone until you show up for yourself?

Rate how full your cup is in each area of your life. Empty 0 -10 Full

Mentally?

Emotionally?

Physically?

Spiritually?

Financially?

Next go through and write down where you want to be. What does that look like? Write down the evidence you need to know that you have reached that number.

Next, look at where you want to go and ask yourself, What's the path of least resistance? Then write down what comes to you. What's the best next step? Write down what comes. If you can take action, do it! If you need more information, ask yourself, what else do I need to know?

Don't force it, allow the answers to come.

THE STORY

October

I surrendered. I stopped everything and asked for guidance. I asked the universe to support me through this process. I was scared. I was vulnerable. I had reached out to many people I thought were my friends in Florida, people I once helped. I was shocked at the reactions I received. I shouldn't have been; I had experienced this before. The more I chose to grow, expand, take responsibility for myself, take responsibility for my actions and stand in my power, the more people eliminated themselves from my life. I got it. It was the crab effect. As we evolve and no longer tolerate behavior we once did, it shines the light on that behavior. When I chose to stop saying it's ok and started saying no, people walked away. The more I got outside of my comfort zone, the more I raised my standards of acceptable behavior. I had experienced real women that have each other's backs. I had experienced people whose words and actions were aligned, who didn't just say unconditional love, they actually embodied it. I learned the difference between those who say it and those who model it. Actions speak so much louder than words. It was amazing to watch and feel people bond over hate and gossip. It was so painful, however it taught me who my real friends were, and are. There were very few people who supported my journey of self-love and self-care, people who actually embraced my authenticity and willingness to fully own my power. I experienced a lot of finger pointing and hate, it was easier to target me than to look in the mirror. It was another gift. I was given an opportunity to practice what I had been learning. Be me, no need to explain, defend, or argue. I chose to rise above and just be. It wasn't easy. These were people I was close to, people I though cared about me, people I cared about and freely gave my energy to. I think what hurt the most was that I was there; in my earlier years I treated people the same way I was being treated. I saw the reflections and karma of where I came from. I was the perfect victim. I used to say unconditional love and acceptance and then judge. I had bonded over the negative. That is why these people were in my life, we were at one point a perfect match. My shadow had been exposed. I owned it and upgraded myself. It was bittersweet to see my growth and be able to rise above my old self and my desire to defend. To defend only pulls me back into the battle powered through fear and need. I had zero interest in returning to that game. I didn't have time for all that gossip and hate, I had to keep my focus on love and being strong for my family.

I released myself from the people, places and things that were no longer serving me. I stopped running and judging and continued consciously choosing the path best for me. I knew something still needed to shift. I needed to be the rock for my mom, for myself. To do so, I needed support. I had no idea what was in store. I felt empty, fearful and alone. I trusted that my answer would come, the universe always provided me exactly what I needed.

It wasn't easy for me to see those earlier reflections of myself. What allowed me to take the high road was the awareness that nothing is personal. Once we evolve to this level of thinking, and ability to see the bigger picture, everything changes. They weren't attacking me; they were reflecting who they were and reminding me where I came from. For example, I had a yogi friend, or so I thought! She promotes love, acceptance, and power. I had reached out to her several times, both while I was away and after returning home, with no response. She had no interest in reconnecting, and then she saw me. Nothing. Nothing until she saw me with a man she had dated. She wanted to talk, needing me to know they dated while I was away. She was visibly upset to the point of shaking. It made no sense to me, she hadn't returned my calls, and they dated, past tense. I asked her how she was and wondered if she wanted to have lunch and catch up, share with me what I was missing. She just got more upset. She wanted details about my relationship with her ex. When I explained it was none of her business, the daggers started to fly. I expressed that I didn't understand the distance between us or her reaction to my friendship with this person. I invited her to talk, in private so we could reestablish a friendship and move past whatever she perceived was happening. She declined and made some interesting accusations before storming away like a child.

I remember being there, so stuck in my story and committed to my perspective that I wasn't open to listening. I was so angry at someone without ever actually talking to them. I can see that version of myself so clearly. It reminded me of the phone calls, people, and places I avoided out of fear of what I may hear. It was easier to ignore it than face the possibility I might be wrong, discovered or exposed. I was so scared of everything, including my real power. Instead, I had a false sense of power and surrounded myself with people who fed my ego. It was the Martyr/Victim mentality. I owned it well and saw the reflection so clearly. I see where a simple conversation could have freed her of so much pain. I respected her choice to be a victim, to be angry at me for not giving her what she wanted and playing into her game. I gained so much appreciation for my willingness to face my past, face other people and be open to hearing other views. I could see how my emotions and snap judgements created so many misconceptions. Misconceptions that kept me stuck and suffering.

It was a gift to know that I healed those parts of me. I had no desire to defend or engage. I was standing there with nothing to hide, nothing to prove, and able to just observe.

Reflection

When we get trapped in emotion and blame others, it only perpetuates the pain. Blame keeps you stuck and powerless. It's a useless emotion. The irony of the entire experience is that if she had been open to talking things through and learning the truth, it may have set her free, on many levels, including the strange accusations. Her outburst taught me so much since I knew her very well. I had a lot of answers that would have freed her from the stories she told me that night. Unfortunately, she was too busy accusing me to be open to anything. I felt her pain, I was stuck in that cycle at one point. All I could do was tell her I love her and let her go. She walked away powerless and angry. Blaming gives your power to that person.

Without blame, there is no need for forgiveness. Every experience is just that, an experience. It's an opportunity for growth, understanding and to better get to know self. It's never about the other person, it's about our own evolution and expansion.

Opportunities

What experiences are you holding onto that keep you powerless?

Where have you created stories without actually gathering all the information?

Are you willing to open up and see another perspective? Ask questions? Gather more information?

What new choices does this new perspective open up for you?

What are you learning about yourself?

MIND VITAMINS

November

I was on Facebook and came across a Mind Vitamins video, leading me to the Mind Vitamins Community. There is where I found so many more amazing videos, uplifting content, messages that resonated with me. Jesse, the creator of the community, captivated my attention right away. I was obsessed with blue eyes. When I visualized the energy and the loving partner I desired I asked for blue eyes, and his eyes were intoxicating. I asked him if I could interview him. The content of his videos was awesome. Everything he talked about was what I had learned in my shamanic training. It reflected the last four years of my journey. I wanted to meet this man. He sent me a link to his AMA (Ask Me Anything) live event.

I watched. I was drawn to him, it was magnetic. His eyes, they were blue and mesmerizing. I could see depth. As I watched the video, he kept asking,

"Why are you here?" "Why are we connected?" "What's your outcome?" "What do you want different?" "What do you want to change?" "What is the opposite of less fear?"

He kept asking questions, great questions. "What if your fear goes away?"

I was mesmerized by him. "What do you want?" He asked this so many times.

"What	*do*	you	want?"
"What	do	*you*	want?"
"What	do	you	*want?*"

I wanted love. I wanted connection. I wanted community. I wanted what I wrote in my intentions...

I intend I see my path unfolding in front of me easily and effortlessly. I intend I always know the best next move for me quickly and intuitively, acting with grace and ease.

I intend I am a lighthouse, a source of power with love, strength and integrity. I intend I am in perfect union with my highest self and the universe as the divine flows through me. I clearly see intent. I respond with compassion, grace and ease. I embrace willingness, humility, and acceptance; acting from integrity and seeing everyone in their highest light.

I intend my book flow through me easily and effortlessly, and is a best seller. I intend the words are of the highest and greatest good as a source of light, hope and inspiration. I intend I am with at least ten clients on a consistent basis. I intend I have a waiting list of new clients who find me easily and effortlessly with desire, finances, time, and willingness to do the required work. I attract clients who appreciate and find value in my services.

I intend my business continue to grow and prosper, making a difference in all lives touched. I intend I am a leader in transformation; inspiring, interviewing, speaking and aligning with other leaders.

I intend I align with my partner easily and effortlessly. I intend we bring out the best in one another. We laugh, love, enjoy and support each other in being the best versions of ourselves. Together we travel, explore, expand and create magic. We make a difference in the world. We focus on each other's strengths, expanding, growing and living to our highest potential.

I intend my life continue to expand, as I am filled with experiences, people, opportunities, love, joy, fun, laughter and abundance on a scale bigger than I could possibly comprehend in this moment. I intend I am filled with fun, outdoor adventurous experiences with amazing people! I intend I am guarded, guided and protected at all times. I AM Happy, Healthy and Whole. I invite the universe to continue to show me how my life can get even more amazing. I intend all this for the highest and greatest good of everyone, everywhere, the universe and myself. So be it and so it is.

I kept watching the video. He reminded me who I was, the me who chose to stop being a victim and own my choices. He talked about being a reflection. I resonated with everything he was saying, especially the ability to no longer see negatives, but to see everything as an expansive experience. It's what I teach to my clients. It was how I look at my life. Each experience is just that, an experience. If the experience was enjoyable, do more of what lead to it; if it was not enjoyable, what did you learn? Either way you gain. He used words that were new to me and opened my mind to a new way to see things. I wanted more.

"When you accept yourself and love yourself unconditionally, you have no regrets. You release judgment, there is no regret." He was asked so many great questions and graciously shared his perspectives. I perceived vulnerability, honesty, gentleness. I saw love, kindness, a man who wanted to free people. A man that had the words, love, and ability to communicate that I had been searching for. He talked about the bully/victim match and how we are always a perfect match. This is all the work I have been doing and continue to do, and Jesse explained it in a way that made sense! His ability to articulate all the things I had experienced and the work I had been doing was priceless. I wanted more.

He said, "I am a reflection of you", I thanked him for being a great mirror.

In his video, he kept talking about his private community, Legacy and a 21 Day Challenge. He shared the next opportunity to join was not till after the next challenge. I had no idea what Legacy was. I went to his website and watched a video of him and another guy, Mike.

The next challenge wasn't for a couple months. I wanted to be in this community. Even though Jesse said we couldn't join, there was an opportunity to buy the package of his and Mike's previous courses. The content looked amazing. There was a link to sign up for Legacy as well, so I followed it and paid, despite what he said. I fully expected to be declined, but I was willing to try.

It was a Saturday. I put my credit card in and released it to the universe, expecting nothing. I walked away. I actually asked my mom if she wanted to go for a walk and get some fresh air and out of our heads for a while. She did.

While we were walking, I couldn't stop thinking about Mike and Jesse. Their energy, their messages, their video. I got chills. I live in Southwest Florida! I was overcome with emotion. I knew I had to be a part of this community. Tears started flowing down my face, my chest started swelling and my body was flushed with emotion. I was feeling so much, releasing something. Opening and expanding. I thanked the universe for whatever was happening and asked for more. I surrendered and said if this is the community I am looking for, please make it happen. I knew I had no control.

In less than 24 hours, I was accepted and part of the community. Mike and Jesse did a live video every Sunday called Sunday Sermon, where they share wisdom and build the community. I was there in time to catch my first Sunday Sermon; it was Jesse's Birthday. I watched as the entire community showered him with love. They had created a surprise birthday video for him, it was beautiful. The difference this man was making in so many lives was evident. All I saw was an outpour of love. I also saw the tears in Jesse's eyes as he watched. I saw a depth. There was no question that this man felt love on a very deep level. He was experiencing exactly was I was seeking, that love and connection. This was the community I was seeking. I was so grateful to be a part of it and to witness such a beautiful expression of love. Jesse represented the love I desired.

I introduced myself to the community and opened up about my current dreams. At that moment, I was wanting to be the next Oprah, interviewing and learning from people. I put that desire out there in the community. I wanted to practice my interviewing and connecting skills. I was received and welcomed with so much love. Many Legends reached out and I was able to do several live interviews. It was awesome! I was meeting and learning about people from all over the world. I connected with people I wouldn't have ever known how to ask for. Again, my intentions were being fulfilled.

I also dove into the content that I had purchased. There was so much to choose from. I was drawn to the community by Jesse, however once there, I seemed to resonate with Mike's teachings more. At that time in my life, Mike and the Power Life Principles were exactly what I needed. Mike shares his stories, his journey through addiction, a suicide attempt, and the challenges of life. He also shares how he managed it, how he rose above and was able to be the lighthouse he is today. I binge watched. I knew the principles. I had heard them before. I even had similar messages in my book, *I'm Sober, Now What?* It didn't matter. I needed Mike in that period of my life. He reminded me who I was and how to keep it simple. He took what I knew and dumbed it down. I was making everything too hard. He really helped me take a few steps back, slow down and breathe. His ability to paint a picture and get the message across in a way a child could understand is so valuable. I watched his videos and cried. Mike was exactly what I needed at that time. He reminded me how far I had come. It was the push I needed to keep going. I cried with gratitude, feeling my body release so much pain. I believed that Jesse was the gateway, the eyes, the draw to lead me to Mike and the community. Throughout much of my journey I followed a path toward a pot of gold, only to discover a kingdom of magic and abundance better than I could have asked for. The more I surrendered, the more amazing life became.

This was a community of people who were encouraged to take responsibility for themselves. People were vulnerable, honest, authentic and real. It was so refreshing. This was the community I had been seeking, the connections I formed were priceless. The day after I joined, Legacy Live was announced. I bought a ticket without hesitation, there was no question I wanted to be there.

Reflections

I went for what I wanted, I didn't listen to Jesse saying there was no option to join, I wanted to be a part of it and tried anyway. I followed my heart and my gut. I found Mike. Mike was exactly what I didn't even know I was looking for. The universe delivered what I didn't know how to ask for. However, I had to surrender, trust and be open to receive.

Opportunities

What do you want right now that you may be hesitating about going after?

Imagine yourself experiencing what you want.

See yourself on the other side, accepted, accomplished, having done whatever it took to have taken the risk to get what you asked for. Write it out…What does it feel like?

Now let go of your expectations of what it should look like. Be open to receive. Be open to the possibilities and allow the path to the magic kingdom to unfold in front of you.

THE POT OF GOLD

November

Plant Medicine has been one of my greatest gifts. Ayahuasca was the first power plant I worked with; it opened me up to a new world. The experience is much like opening Pandora's box, once you look inside, you can't un-know. It's not a magic pill or shortcut, it's a passage. Choosing the path requires work. It's a deeply personal journey that requires much self-reflection. This was my first introduction to Love, source love and divine connection.

After working with Ayahuasca for a while, I was guided to learn more. That is when I found Susun and started my training. I entered my first Shamanic Herbal Apprenticeship. I have been training for a few years now. I went on a journey and learned the power of working with all plant medicines on multiple levels. There is as much medicine and wisdom in the weeds and everyday herbs as there is in poisonous plants. It has been an incredible journey that brought me back full circle. Just like Mike reminded me that there is sometimes more to gain from the simplicity, the plants were teaching me the same thing. They are miraculous teachers if we choose to listen and understand.

Through my shamanic teachings, I was gifted the opportunity to facilitate ceremonies. Along with the ceremonial work I supported all who worked with me through their integration process. The awakening is the easy part, integrating what was learned and rewriting your reality to create a new future is where the work comes in. It was a lot for many people. It takes a couple weeks for the energy to close down and if proper precautions are not set up, the entire experience can create an adverse effect rather than a breakthrough. I felt a shift coming. There were some people in the circle that leaned more toward profit than the safety of participants. I saw carelessness and I could not be a part of it any longer. I walked away. The medicine showed me how to channel the energy and get similar results without myself or a client needing to ingest anything. I was taken on a journey by the spirits of all the plants I had worked with, each teaching me how they can assist the process if the clients are open and willing to the healing. It was safer for the client, and easier to integrate into busy lives. People were still releasing stuck energy and experiencing massive breakthroughs. The recovery and integration process catered to people who had jobs, responsibilities and families and were unable to take off a week or two. They were still able to have powerful results and ease back into their responsibilities gracefully. It was beautiful. The results kept getting better and it allowed me to stay within my integrity.

I had been working this way for about a year when I received the call to come home, home to the medicine. The first invitation came from a woman I will call Maggie. Maggie had experienced one of my sessions. She had huge breakthroughs and released herself from much suffering. Maggie had been going to a medicine church that worked with addiction and PTSD. She wanted me to help them open a branch locally. I was so excited; this was my dream! To facilitate and help people integrate. I was sure this was my path. I was sure that this was everything I had asked for. I believed that my integrity of walking away from the medicine and the circle I was in, was the best thing I could have done for the best interest of the people and clients. My commitment to only operating for the highest good of all was leading me to like-minded opportunities. I was invited to spend a weekend with Maggie and meet the team she had been working with. We were not scheduled to go for a couple months, the weekend right before Legacy Live. The church was in the middle of Florida, so I planned to drive there and then go from there to Texas.

Meanwhile...

Minh, the man I started the medicine journey with, invited me to come with him to the Santo Daime Church he attended. He had been going for a couple years and always talked about this amazing family, how much he learned and how much he loved them. I couldn't wait to go. I wanted to go. I was excited to go. I was ready to reconnect and thought it would be a great opportunity before starting the journey of facilitating again.

Minh was not only my medicine friend, but also like a brother to me. He is one of the few people that knew me before I got sober. We both had breakthroughs and committed to becoming the best versions of ourselves. Our growth and paths took us in different directions that would often intertwine. We always made a point of staying in touch and checking in on each other. We often reached out to each other in times of self-question, knowing that we always had each other's back. I knew he had my best interest at heart, and he knew I had his as well. It was a beautiful friendship. We were both so excited to do the work together again. It really was full circle! I was so excited to meet his spiritual family.

The plans were made and everything was falling into place. I was going to get reacquainted with the medicine through Minh and be fully prepared to help build a leg of the other church if that was how it all worked out. I was open, excited and willing.

The church and the Legacy community were my fuel to stay strong for my family.

I went with Minh to the Santo Daime Church. Wow! This was the first time I worked with plant medicine in this way. There was no shaman, and there was no darkness. We did the work with the lights on, fully present, and together. The work was collective; everyone had a part. It was very different than everything I had known. It wasn't just one or two people to lead and carry the ceremony, it was about everyone doing their part. The teachings were powerful, both from the medicine and the members. I was learning so much. I was letting go of so much. I was open to this new way of being.

The community was exactly as he had described. After ceremonies, it was like a family reunion. Music, joy, food, connection. I felt so much love and support. These people embraced me, and welcomed me. The women reminded me of my experience with Lis in New York. They were accepting, loving, generous, and wanted to know me. It was exactly what I was looking for and what I needed.

I went to several ceremonies over the next couple months leading up to my visit with the other church and then Texas. I was falling in love with the people, they were becoming like family. The more time I spent with this family, the more I started to question everything. I began wondering how I could be a part of both churches. They are both so different. One I would be leading, facilitating, integrating and feeding what I thought was my dream role. The other I would be part of a team, a collective where everyone is responsible for their own healing. I had support. I had a lot to think about and knew I was excited to explore the opportunity.

Meanwhile in Legacy, I was on an emotional rollercoaster. I felt like I was living in a multidimensional reality. There was more to Jesse....I felt something. Something intense that was familiar and foreign at the same time. There were so many contradicting signs.

I was shifting so much internally with ceremony and Legacy. The emotions were extreme and I was starting to second guess everything I thought I knew.

Reflections

I believed that my path was unfolding easily and effortlessly before me as requested. Life was good! I was experiencing love, joy, community and connections. Opportunities were presenting themselves everywhere, so many choices. I was making conscious choices and open and excited to see what was next!

I was so grateful for Minh, as one of the few that really encouraged my growth, my sobriety and my transformation. I also appreciated his girlfriend, Carolina for welcoming me. She played a powerful role in his inviting me to the church and helping me find comfort in the community.

Opportunities

Is there a path you have been walking that you just know is the best path for you?

How open are you to the universe showing you options?

How open are you to seeing possibilities that you may not even know exist?

It's kind of like that pot of gold I talked about that actually lead me to the magic kingdom.

TAKING RISKS

December

Every time Jesse asked, "what do you want?", I connected to my heart and thought, "love. I want love." I was open to him being the man I was seeking until I joined Legacy. After resonating with Mike and Power Life Principles, I let that thought go. I focused on myself and what I needed to do. I focused on my family, the church, and really working toward building my business. I needed to choose a direction and stick to it.

The more I got involved with Legacy, the more I watched Jesse's videos, the more I was drawn toward him. His use of words pulled me in. I shared earlier in my journey that there was no question my path involved discovering my truth and the use of words. My entire journey over the last few years was to discover how my words created my reality and I have been on a mission to discover new ways to rewrite reality. I work with clients to rewrite their story. Story medicine is a passion of mine. I had rewritten my path and revised it many times. The more I learned, the less I realized I knew. I was so open and hungry for new perspectives. Jesse had many. He was a wordsmith with the ability to invoke emotion powerfully, and with deliberate intention.

His use of story medicine was engaging. When he told his stories, he was telling mine. When he spoke of others, he did so with respect.

I perceived this man to be: open minded, willing to travel, loving, with good intention to awaken and shine a light for others, adaptable, free to express himself, desiring to empower others, etc. I was open to him being the partner I was seeking and the possibly that universe was guiding me directly to him.

After finishing Mike's videos, I dove into Jesse's meditation series. It was very much in line with what I had been practicing. It reminded me of New York when I visualized and felt the energy and experiences I wanted. His process added more questions and took me deeper. I went back to the drawing board and really sank into myself, getting clarity on what I want. I believed that he was the gateway to deeper self-discovery.

The more I meditated and asked myself "what do I want", the more my chest swelled and the more clarity I gained reinforcing that I wanted love. I was ready to allow a partner in again. I wanted to experience what a healthy partnership was. I wanted to experience what it felt like to be supported, honored, respected and cherished by a man. I have so much to give, I wanted a person to give it to. And the more I asked the universe to show me my partner, the more signs I received pointing me toward Jesse.

I was really going through a dark spot. I had to surrender again and asked for a sign. I was crying, hurting, needing support. I cried out, "If this is real, if he is actually the one, please give me a sign!" I cried and let it go. That night, I woke up in the middle of the night. I had been sleeping hard, but something directed me to open my phone and look at Facebook. Against my logical judgment I did. I had posted a video that day, crying and sharing a story of something I was experiencing. I had shared many videos and many stories. However, this was the first one that Jesse ever acknowledged. I had accepted the fact that Legacy was a gift of community with no expectation of ever really interacting with Jesse. He rarely commented on posts and was actually traveling most of the time I was a member. So when I cried for a sign, and both Jesse and Mike commented on a video, that kept me open. I was emotional and confused.

I thanked the universe. I cried and said if he is the man for me, please help me. I expressed that his beard completely grossed me out, but if he really was the one, then I give me a sign. I was so emotional, grateful for the message and open to whatever the universe had in store for me. I rolled over and cried myself back to sleep. When I woke up the next morning he posted a new picture; he had shaved his beard. I was paralyzed with chills running through my body.

That same day, Jesse did a live video, announcing he too was ready to include a partner in his life. He was ready to share with a special woman. The way he spoke of women was so respectful. He never dishonored, named or blamed anyone. He shared from his heart, his perfectives and what he learned. I was convinced the universe was bringing us together. He read his letter to the universe, the one requesting his ideal match. And then he announced, he'd met her. She would be joining him on his world tour and then be at Legacy Live with all of us. My heart sank. I was so confused. I asked the universe to please help me understand why the mixed messages, what was happening to me?

I let it go and went to one of the works with Minh. I desperately needed help, answers, support, and clarity. I got it. I realized I asked for the man of my dreams, I asked to be magnetically drawn to him. What I learned from listening to Jesse is that I didn't ask for it to be reciprocal. Jesse was the man of my dreams; however, I was not the woman of his. The way he stated his request and his use of words was so eloquent. I studied it. During the work that night, I sent him love and gratitude for all I learned from him. It was painful, however I accepted that the entire experience was to free me and teach me. I accepted that Jesse was my teacher, not potential partner. I was so grateful for the breakthrough and assumed that I am now free to align with my partner. I had better words and the awareness to ask for a lover who loves me back!

I was excited for Jesse and looking forward to seeing where this all took me next.

I let go and focused on the content with Legacy, and kept moving forward. I was happy to have clarity on Jesse's role in my life. I was happy his journey was able to shed light on how I can make better use of my words. I was finding so much support and strength in all the other Legends. The group was priceless. The connections, the growth, the experience was generating so much expansion. Things were aligning again.

I went back to my meditations and visualizations. I tweaked the words and put my energy toward creating my own happiness. I kept asking the universe to magnetize me to my partner, to show me, to guide me. Every time I did, I was led to Jesse. I kept saying, he's taken, show me my ideal partner. Again, Jesse. I let go and accepted that I am not meant to align with my lover at this time. I knew it wasn't Jesse and had to just let go of everything.

Soon after, Jesse announced that it did not work out with the woman he was guided to. My heart sank. I couldn't help but wonder if we really were meant to be. I started getting my hopes up. I asked for more signs. He updated a profile picture, there was a red feather on his shirt, it was exactly like the tattoo on my arm.

There was more… and I surrendered. I thought it was all so I could let go of the need and be the partner he desired. I believed the universe was freeing me so that I was in a place that was aligned with Jesse. I was so obsessed with him, the signs, the emotion. It was so real for me. I believed that hearing he found a lover was a gift for me, to free me from the need. I was surprised at how happy I was for him and how grateful I was to learn how to word my desires in a more useful way. The more I appreciated Jesse for what I was learning and let go of him, the stronger he appeared to me. It was so powerful and so confusing.

The red feather, along with all the other signs I was getting made no sense to me. I accepted he wasn't the one, yet was still being magnetically drawn to him. And to be perfectly honest, deep down I was hopeful that maybe he really was the one. I didn't know what to do. The feelings were more intense than anything I had ever experienced.

I didn't tell anyone. I was so embarrassed and ashamed. I felt so stupid. I was in love with a man who barely knew I existed. I was obsessed. I had witnessed this behavior in other women and been baffled by it. I had no idea how to deal with this, and it was so painful. It was so real.

I asked myself what I would tell a client to do. I would tell them to be honest. One of the things I learned from my sobriety was that secrets keep us sick. I had to tell someone. I had to work through this. I asked for another sign. One of the things Jesse teaches is to send appreciation videos, so I decided to record him a private video and send it to him. I recorded it, it was 21 minutes and 12 seconds long. 21.12. To me, that was a sign. My birthday is 12/21 and every time I see the combination, I know I am on the right path. Numbers are one of the ways the universe has always spoken to me. It was my first language. So without watching the video and without hesitation, I sent it.

I sent it through Mike, asking him to forward it since Jesse and I weren't friends. Mike agreed. I had several little conversations with Mike in Messenger. He was always kind, compassionate and a man of integrity. I sent it and let it go.

I never heard a word. To this day, I have no idea if Jesse received it or watched it. I can only hope not! I cried and poured my soul out for twenty minutes expressing my love and how I am driving to Texas because I believe that I am in love with him. Seriously? Looking back, what was I thinking? This man didn't know me and I didn't know him. I was attached to the idea I created of him. I thought I may have possibly found the man of my dreams and, I vomited on him! I was so disgusted with myself and then I laughed. I realized that I had nothing left. I stopped judging and shaming myself and asked what I would tell a client. I would tell them; You put yourself out there, you were vulnerable and you were honest. If this man doesn't see that part of you, he doesn't deserve you. This isn't about him; this is about you. You were brave, and you will never wonder what if. He may be the one, he may not, it doesn't matter. You showed up authentically and you learned something powerful. Next time, you will do it differently. You learned. It hurt, it didn't turn out the way you wanted, but you got so much out of this experience. You will never wonder what if. Man, I must say, I love my self-talk. I love myself. I love my ability to be raw, vulnerable and honest. I love that I am able to move through the fear and show up authentically. I was so excited and I wondered what else was there.

Reflections

I chose to move through my fear. When my desired results were not achieved, I chose to let go of shame and feeling stupid. I asked for signs and I trusted those signs. Looking back, I would do it all again. Why? I learned from it. I will never wonder what if and for me that is the point. I tried and that's all any of us can do.

I may not have received the love I desired from Jesse, however, I did receive it from myself. I was able to laugh at myself, accept myself and enjoy the journey. That's a breakthrough in itself.

Self-love and self-acceptance are essential to the process. True freedom comes from not needing anyone else's approval. I was there! I loved myself for being willing to take the risk. I loved myself for being able to laugh at my silly antics. I honored myself for sharing authentically.

None of this was about Jesse, it was about me doing what I needed to do for me. I was loving, honoring and supporting myself the way I was searching for it to come from someone else! Priceless!

Opportunities

Think of a time you took a risk. One that didn't turn out the way you wished.

Are you carrying shame, blame and guilt? What would you tell your best friend if they were in your shoes?

Write out your new story, the one that highlights your courage!

What did you learn?

How did that risk empower you?

UNEXPECTED SIGNS

February

I was ready to let go of Legacy, of Jesse, and skip the live event. I was convinced he was a gift to free me. I took ownership of the fact that my obsession and perceived love was all showing me where I could love myself more. I projected onto him what I needed to give myself. I was grateful and I was ready to get off the roller coaster. It was time to visit the Ayahuasca Church and gather more information for my path. I would decide at the end of the weekend if I was continuing on to Texas.

I drove three hours to spend the weekend at the Ayahuasca Church. I loved the Santo Daime and needed this experience to make a best decision for me. It was a beautiful experience. The Ayahuasca church absolutely cares about each participant. They had an intense screening process, making sure that everyone's health was in check before allowing participation. They really focused on education, follow up care, and helping people integrate. There was no question of the integrity of this church and the team running it. Both churches deeply cared for safety and well-being of the people first.

I had now experienced two very different options. I had a lot to think about. I had seen two very powerful churches, both offering very different paths. Both had benefits and drawbacks. I needed time to figure out what path was best for me.

I had debated not going to Texas, thinking I already received the messages I was called there for. I was in love with the idea of magically connecting with the man of my dreams. In reality I had never actually even spoke to this man or been acknowledged by him, so there was really no loss. I realized that what I fell in love with really was what I projected on him.

I reflected. I went back to what it was that I thought I loved. It started with a picture of Jesse squatting down, face to face with a little boy. I believe the picture was in a third world country, possibly Ethiopia. The connection and sparkle in both of their eyes was priceless. All I saw was a desire to understand, love and be present. I saw real connection.

I then remembered a video I saw online of him bouncing on his butt dancing. There were many people around, it looked like a bar. Again, this was that same trip he was on. His face and an older gentleman's face were lit up. It was dark, however their smiles, their joy, their love radiated. I could feel it.

Then there were pictures of him holding baby goats! I spent days at Susun's milking goats, herding goats and learning from goats. I even witnessed them being born. I remembered a picture of him by a huge tree, in the middle of I don't know where. It reminded me of home. It reminded me of my Willow Tree. It reminded me of my journey, love of trees and connection. When I looked at Jesse, I attached the story of a man spreading love, connecting deeply to people and doing his best to leave people feeling more inspired and loved after being in his presence.

I soon learned that he went on this trip to understand what it felt like to be the minority. He was seeking to understand. He was seeking to see the world through a new perspective. His journey reminded me of my own. I fell in love with that version of Jesse. I fell in love with myself, my desire to understand, connect, and love. I realized I was in love with everything he was doing because it reminded me of the journey I was on.

He reminded me. He wasn't scared of the unknown, of getting dirty, of exploring. He embraced adventure, the unknown, and getting out of his comfort zone. I had been on this solo journey and saw him as someone that I would love to travel with. I saw him as someone who embraced experience, valued people, learning, and loving. When I watched him, I projected a man who cared more about making a difference, uplifting another, and being more about change than about money and power. I chose to see a man who lived the life I was living. A man that was fully present, engaged, vulnerable, willing and humble.

I believed he went deep and connected on a level that many never experience. I recognized his soul in a way that I cannot explain, a depth, a shift, the transformation. At least, this was my perception and projection at the time. I fell in love with the story I attached to his experience. Looking back, I can see how unfair this was to him. However, at the time, I was unclear of what was happening, it was all still too fresh. I was so emotional. I knew what I was seeing in him was really about me; my desire to connect that deeply, memories of the journey I had just gone on and the connections I made. I connected so deeply and the love I experienced was so powerful. I was reflecting on my journey and projecting it onto him. I figured I no longer needed to go, he wasn't the man of my dreams, but a powerful illusion to guide me back to me. I was really considering going home when I asked for guidance.

I was sitting outside the church when I looked around for answers. I just started laughing...there I was, in the Ayahuasca church in the middle of Florida, surrounded by mind-bending art and multidimensional décor and one pillow with the state of Texas on it. I was being called and needed to continue along this path that did not make sense to me. I was an emotional mess at this point. I knew I had to keep going.

I surrendered, trusted and headed to Texas.

I had so many emotions running through my body as I drove to Texas. As much as I knew that I projected onto Jesse, deep down there was a part of me that still wanted my fantasy to be real. I wanted love and was ready for a partner. There were so many signs leading me to believe he could be the one. And on top of the signs, I felt pulled. It was as if I was in a vacuum or wind tunnel, being drawn to him. Then I thought about it. I asked to be magnetically drawn to the man I had asked the universe for. I felt that pull in every cell in my body. I was being pulled toward what? The man that I had sent an embarrassing video? The man that wanted nothing to do with me? I totally understood why. I was having an experience all my own and I felt like I was nuts. I looked at the silly things I had done. I wondered how I was going to face him. I had to laugh at myself. I looked back over the last few months as I drove.

Reflections

Jesse often said, need nothing, appreciate everything. That was what I set out to do last April when I left. I wanted to move through life with only my intuition and trust. To fully experience life without attachment, without need. I fell in love with the version of myself I had been and was becoming. He really was a perfect mirror.

Opportunities

Who in your life captivates your attention?

What about them are you drawn to? Write down their name and then write down all the reasons you adore them. Allow yourself to flow and fully appreciate having them in your life.

Do this with as many people as possible. Then reflect on your why. This is you. Welcome to all the ways you can fall deeper in love with yourself!

WITNESSING YOURSELF

February

I arrived in Texas a day earlier than I expected. I was able to join the group I rented a house with as many of them were already there. There were so many people, traveling from all over the world. Everyone who had arrived early decided to gather for dinner and to finally meet face to face. It was dreamlike, there had been so much hype and now we were finally all together. I had so much fun really getting to know all these Legends that I had only met on line. These people were another family to me, they had been witnessing and supporting my growth. I had been witnessing and supporting theirs as well. This was more of what I asked for. Everyone saw each other's light and lifted each other up. I wanted to be a lighthouse and I was. I was also surrounded with them. I realized this was why I needed to drive to Texas, to connect with an army of lighthouses. There was so much love, talent, and inspiration among this group. There was no competition, only people who truly wanted the best for each other. I was feeling good. I was so happy I chose to show up.

After dinner, people all went separate ways. I went back to the house. I had my tools with me since I came right from ceremony. I brought them in and shared an experience with those who were interested. I played the bowls and my drum. We did some fun work with candles, energy and seeing the depth of each other. I opened up some doors for people to see deeper parts of themselves and others. It was nice. Then something hit me, an energy. I was being pulled to release it. It was an energy that felt unfamiliarly familiar. I had to get permission from the people carrying it. We all had to surrender, they had to be willing to let it go. They were, and in doing so, I released myself. Something happened that night. I felt emptier and more disconnected. I knew the release was a good thing, however I wasn't sure what it was. Instantly the people I was once drawn to shifted. Everything shifted. There was no question this was part of my path. I cleared my energy and we all went to bed.

The next morning, the shift was obvious. I felt so much lighter. I did my yoga and my meditation and the rest of my morning ritual. I then enjoyed a great day leading up to the meet and greet kickoff for the weekend. My nerves were running rampant knowing I would finally be done with this delusion; I was so ready to meet Jesse and be done with whatever I was experiencing. I was so uncomfortable.

We were at the restaurant for the kickoff party. More and more Legends showed up, the crowd was forming, the excitement was rising. Many were just arriving and connecting for the first time. The weekend was definitely here. As the night built, there he was. He had on the shirt, the one with the red feather. Seeing him in person for the first time, the energy, the intensity, the group, it was surreal. Everyone was taking pictures with Jesse and Mike, thanking them, getting to know them. I said hello to Mike and took a picture with him, however something stopped me from nearing Jesse. A voice in my head said wait. So I did. I went internal and listened to what I was feeling, hearing, and connected to the messages I was receiving.

Something shifted. I felt paralyzed. I just stood there, feeling so disconnected. I was in a room full of people and felt so incredibly alone. I watched. I listened. I felt like a child, insecure and off. I just looked at Jesse, his eyes and that shirt. The closer I got, the heavier I became. It was like walking into a wind tunnel, I was being forced back. I needed to walk away.

I pulled myself together and connected with some of the other Legends. I let go of whatever was happening and got present. I ended the evening with some pretty amazing connections. I swapped stories and got to know another energy worker. We talked about all the downloads and visions we were both experiencing. It put me at ease. I knew there was something bigger happening, something that may not be fully clear for a while. I connected to my inner compass and trusted. I was able to show up and be present with the people who had been supporting me through my family challenges and my expansion.

The next morning the event really escalated. I was guided not to approach or go near Jesse. I was to witness what was happening and just be as present as possible. I felt heavy. I felt the anticipation of something, I just had no idea what. I did my best to be present, helped by sitting with the crew I was staying with. The roofer was hilarious and really pulled me out of my head. I appreciated his kindness and humor so much! I was able to enjoy the day and be present.

The energy was intense. Jesse really brought a powerful charge to the room. I could feel my crown chakra going crazy, it felt like there were fireworks on my head. I was getting downloads so fast I could barely keep up. I thought I was going insane. I just sat there, feeling, witnessing, doing what I was guided to do. I had no idea what the heck was happening, and yet I did, all at the same time. I felt like I was in a dream, I couldn't move, yet I was so present. It was so bizarre.

I had some really private and meaningful conversations with many people. I was present for many conversations I was not a part of. It was fascinating to learn how the transmission sent from Jesse and Mike was being received, perceived, interpreted and repeated. Everyone was having their own experience based on their own reality. I learned so much about people by how they received and regurgitated the information. Some were angry and rejected the information, some were skeptical, yet open, others easily accepting it as their truth. Everyone was there for their own reasons, each choosing what was of value to them. The conversations were interesting and informative.

I knew I was there for something powerful and trusted what I was being guided to do. I was feeling so out of alignment, so outside of my being. Everything and nothing made sense all at the same time. I had to just surrender. It was as if I was in a bubble, watching myself. I could see myself there, yet I was only allowed minimal contact. I felt like I was sitting back reviewing my life as it was unfolding. Looking back, I realize I was rewriting my life, traveling through time and space, and that minimal contact was to allow a new outcome.

Day two I spent sitting with an entirely different group of people. I sat next to Cher. I didn't really know her and had not really been connected to her. I was surprised when she invited me to sit next to her, admitting she was very turned off by me at first. Neither of us really knew why she wanted me next to her that second day, however we soon found out. Something powerful happened between us that day, something that allowed us to both see differently; a huge shift that was scary and exciting to us both. We've talked about it since, however in that moment, we both just sat there. We knew there was an upgrade and we both needed to recalibrate and integrate.

We took many breaks. I cleared my energy, grounded, went out for some fresh air and silence. There was a magical tree in the courtyard with graceful energy. I was drawn to that spirit and just stood with it, absorbing the love of both the spirit and the earth. It was like being home. A nice break before more fireworks were about to go off!

Jesse took a break from presenting and Mike was talking. He was sharing about feeling alone and disconnected. He was talking about how when you are willing to walk alone to honor your path and explore the leading edge it can be a very lonely path. I was resonating with everything he was saying. I was so present with him, shaking my head, really feeling everything he was saying. I felt so alone and misunderstood many times.

The more I expanded and grew, the more alone I felt. I sat there, shaking my head. I felt something, it was strong, I shifted my gaze from Mike to see what it was. As I looked over, our eyes met. Jesse and I made eye contact; he was mirroring me. I was paralyzed. I knew we both were so deeply connected to Mike's message, feeling the words. I just stared. I couldn't even smile. I finally made eye contact with the man of my dreams and I was expressionless and so present in that moment. And then it happened, I felt a shock. It felt like a cattle prod to my heart. The electric jolt was like a surge to my chest and then dissipated up and down my spine. I had never felt anything like it. Jesse smirked and looked away. I have no idea what face I made, if any. I was in shock. In that 30 seconds, time stood still and it felt like 30 years for me. What was it about this man? All I knew was the next download I got was keep your distance, if you touch him, you will explode! What the heck? I knew there was something more and I would not get the answers at that time. I had to just trust. After that I had an out of body experience where I saw multiple versions of myself in that room, having different experiences. It was incredible. I learned so much and couldn't share it with anyone. I wanted to talk to him so desperately, and I couldn't. I just kept hearing you will regret it, it's not time. Leave the energy alone. I knew there was more, however I had no idea what it was.

Against all my logical thinking, I trusted the messages I was getting. I had to let go of whatever this was or wasn't. I fought to get present. Fifteen minutes later, Jesse announced he was hopping on a plane after the event to have dinner with a special lady in LA. My heart sank. He really was my perfect mirror, both chasing the opportunity for love.

The rest of the day was a blur. I was getting visions, messages, downloads. I needed to process what was happening. I opened the door to a couple people I thought would understand and be able to help me talk it out. I closed that door quickly. Nothing felt right. I needed to just let it all go until I left. I had a long drive back to Florida to figure it all out!

I felt like I was in quicksand, the more I tried to connect, the farther away I was. The words coming out of my mouth didn't match the thoughts in my head. I had been here before; I was forcing it. I needed to just walk away. There was so much energy there, so many people. I could feel them, their vibrations, their feelings, their intentions. I smell everything. I feel everything. My senses were on overload. I went out and smudged myself to clear whatever wasn't mine and sat with the tree. I needed to find me again.

That evening was the farewell dinner and goodbye party. I was there, physically anyway. I couldn't dance or get into it. I was off. I watched everyone having a blast and I just felt numb, heavy, and like an observer of someone else's life, another version of my own. I looked around to say goodbye, no one seemed to notice me. I was glad. Then I looked up and saw Nicole. She was sitting there by herself enjoying the moment. I was drawn to her, so I went to talk to her. She was nothing like I expected. Nicole needed a ride and I was happy to provide it. I was ready to go.

As Nicole and I talked, we made plans to get together the next morning. Turns out she was looking for some energy work and I just happen to be the one she was drawn to. We set it up and she came over the next morning. From that day forward, Nicole has been one of my greatest allies and friends. She was definitely one of the reasons I was there!

Reflections

At the time, it was so hard to just witness, to trust, to observe. I desperately wanted to connect to people. I had connected to many of these people and had deep appreciation for them. I wanted something completely different than I was being guided to do. I wanted to talk to Jesse. I wanted to feel something different. However, I chose to trust my internal guidance system. I worked really hard to create a language with my guides, I needed to honor what I was receiving.

I chose to surrender and trust the process. It was not easy.

Smudging often and clearing my energy helped. Sage and sweet grass are my favorites that I travel with. For those who don't know what smudging is, it is the process of burning sacred herbs or resins to shift or clear our energy.

Opportunities

Are you prepared to handle chaos, confusion and uncertainty?

How do you handle discomfort?

Meditation is one of the strongest tools, in my experience, to prepare for uncomfortable situations.

Connect to the breath. The breath teaches us so much. Your thoughts follow your breath. Shallow, quick breathing usually accompanies anxiety, fear, racing thoughts and a very active mind. If you can slow your breathing, you can slow your thoughts. It's important to slow down, be present and pay attention to what you are feeling. Slowing the mind allows clarity.

Try breathing in for a count of 5,

Hold your breath for a count of 5,

Release for a count of 5,

Hold out for a count of 5.

Do this 5 times and see what happens. Observe your mind before and after.

FEEDING THE FEAR

February

I was scheduled to stay another night in Texas, however I couldn't leave fast enough. I knew I got exactly what I came for, and needed quiet. I desperately wanted to be alone. As I drove away, the decompression and silence were priceless. I felt the heaviness lifting.

I just wanted to be home.

I had so much to reflect on. I wasn't ready to process. I cleared my mind and just drove. I wasn't sure what to focus on; My family, Legacy or the Churches. I was too close to all of it. I knew from experience that I had to distance myself before I could look at any of it objectively.

I had talked to mom; Don took a turn for the worse. I needed to get out of my head. I needed a friend.

I called a friend. I was excited to check in with him. We had been working together for a while and had some tremendous breakthroughs. Right before I left, we decided to trade services. He was a former client, turned friend. When he hired me, he expressed a desire to be Gandalf, the great white wizard of love, and to really promote healing. He wanted it bad. He wanted to own his power. Throughout our time working together, he had so many shifts. He was able to rewrite several stories and free himself from years of bondage. His business grew, his confidence grew, and his life was expanding. It was beautiful. We did some really deep work and ended up becoming quite good friends.

As Gandalf grew, he started working at a healing center that I worked for a couple years prior. I never said a word about my experience there or why I left. It was my experience and I left. There was no reason to bring it up. My gut reaction was, "Oh no!", however he didn't ask and I didn't interfere. I supported his experience and prayed it would be much better than my own.

He had been there for a couple months when he started shifting in a different direction. The progress was fading and old patterns were resurfacing. I figured this had a lot to do with why he wanted an energy session and deep clearing again. I didn't ask. We made a deal and I trusted that the answers would be revealed just as they always had been. I did the work on him before I left and he talked me into waiting until his next group course to fulfill his part of the deal. He was planning it at the healing center. I was apprehensive, but trusted him to be the person he said he wanted to be and follow through. He asked me for the opportunity to hold space and create real healing and breakthroughs. This was that opportunity. I allowed him to position himself to stand in his power and facilitate a group experience at this place of employment. I was open to being wrong about how I felt and I was open to the possibility that everyone involved had grown. It was a healing center; I chose to have faith that they truly wanted to elevate and honor the message they promote.

I did ask Gandalf to get permission from the owner for me to attend, before I performed my services. He assured me he talked to her and it was all set, I was welcome as his guest in honor of our trade. My gut in that moment was telling me otherwise, however I chose to give Gandalf and his word the benefit of the doubt. Gandalf convinced me he wanted to be powerful and act with love and integrity, this was his opportunity. I was willing to honor the work we started and hold that space with him. I trusted him.

Before I left, I provided the agreed upon services. He was going through something and needed help. We cleared all kinds of stuff. I then charged some tools and products to support the integration and left them with him.

I was so excited to hear his voice and hear about all the positive changes in his life. He was really shifting, growing and gaining. He was sharing how everything was falling into place for him. The transformation was beautiful and I was so happy for him.

And then he told me... "Willow, you are not welcome to come to the healing."

"What?" I was in shock.

He admitted that he never even asked if I could come. He never shared that we were working together and how much that experience helped him. He lied to me about getting permission for me to come. He lied about everything, accepted my services and then made excuses. I felt sick.

He never asked about my experience there or looked for clarity. Instead he heard gossip, accepted it as truth and brought it back to me.

My response, "So you work for a healing center that won't allow you to honor your word, has rules about who is allowed to attend healings, gossips about past clients and employees, and this is ok with you?"

He was ok with it. I took the information and said goodbye. It was painful and I had a long drive to reflect on this now too.

He taught me so much about himself that day. He since has apologized for not having my back or honoring his word. He said he "needed the center", they were feeding him clients. Again, that taught me so much. I remember being in a place where I felt I needed someone else to feed me. I remember feeling powerless and weak. It was bittersweet for me. I appreciated that moment so much. My intuition was confirmed. I knew I left there for a reason. I knew allowing this to play out would expose something I needed to see. I didn't anticipate the truth I learned. I was grateful to learn that Gandalf was willing to sell himself and compromise his integrity prior to allowing him in my energy. The teachings and experience can only hold the power and integrity of the facilitator. He compromised and gave his away. I wouldn't, then or now, and that is why I left. I was so grateful. I honored my commitment to Gandalf by being willing to hold that space and I honored my love to myself for being strong enough to let it all go with love. I saw what I needed to see.

When life is the hardest, you really find out who your friends are. I had a long drive to reflect, and I started with Gandalf. I had called him to get out of my head and was thrust back into it. As I looked back over our time together, I noticed a pattern. There are no secrets about me having a past and being in recovery. I have transformed my life. Yet more times than not, Gandalf would tell me about gossip he heard about me. He even witnessed a ceremonial event that I created to allow him to step into his power. At the event, he witnessed a woman experience a huge healing and thank me for the space. I never saw her again. He shared that he ran into her and she spoke ill of me. He couldn't wait to tell me. I uncovered his pattern! What a gift!

What Gandalf taught me is how he disables people to create leverage. He desperately wanted power, yet was so powerless. He attached himself to women in their power, attempted to hurt them by sharing gossip and then tried to console them. It was his MO. He used black magic. He loved to share gossip and pretend it was because he cared. He would act as though he "has your back" while saying hateful things. Then when the person is reflecting, trying to make sense of what he was saying, he would position and leverage himself as the healer. It was so clear to me. He hurt people to try to heal them. I don't believe it was intentional, it was how her learned to connect and feel important.

I am so grateful for that experience. I was able to see where I did the same thing in the past. I attempted to bond with people over sharing what I heard. This was all before I learned the power of words and magic. Gossip is black magic; it's using the word to hurt people. When speaking ill of another, it's a curse. It was all before I loved myself and realized that people who love themselves don't go around spreading gossip and hurting others. When you repeat gossip, you are not doing someone a favor, you are cursing them. Shutting the gossip down is what people in their power and work in the light do. They stick up for others and shed light on the opportunity to rise above and be kind to each other.

Gandalf taught me how to spot black magic instantly. He modeled how he plays people against each other to make himself the hero. I released myself from him and his debt to me. I celebrated the clarity and was so happy he exposed himself and this behavior to me. It freed me from so much and really allowed me to see how people who operate from fear are vulnerable to being used. I was there once.

Reflection

For me this confirmed my intuition; how trusting it really exposed so many layers of how words can really heal or hurt another. It shed so much light on everything I had been learning and doing. I celebrated how far I had come and how much I had learned. I was so grateful I walked away and chose self-love and to honor myself and everyone else. This was another fight I had no reason to enter. It was another opportunity to see the hate and rise above.

I had to be willing to get hurt to see. I had to risk exposing myself for the truth to come out. I was willing to walk into my past, face it head on. I was willing to be wrong and I was open to the possibility of this healing center truly caring about healing.

It felt so good to have nothing to hide and nothing to prove. It felt even better knowing that my intuition was dead on, both then and now.

It was also another reminder that people are always teaching you who they are, what kind of friend they are and what kind of person they are. If someone gossips to you, they will gossip about you. People who love themselves don't go around hurting others. People who love themselves don't defend, engage, or repeat gossip. They transmute that energy on the spot.

Gossip is like a deadly infection, venom, nothing good comes from it.

Opportunities

How do you handle gossip?

Do you believe everything you hear or trust your own experience?

What are your experiences teaching you?

What are the people you engage with teaching you?

MAKING DECISIONS

February/March

Choices. At one point in my life, I didn't think I had a choice. I did what I was told. I did what was expected. I followed the societal rules. I was so conscious not to rock the boat, as the saying goes. I accepted what I was told by anyone I perceived as authority. I questioned nothing and was scared to say a word when things didn't seem right. I lived in fear and survival mode for so long.

Does any of this sound familiar?

Are there times you wanted to speak up, but you didn't?

Is there something you may be holding back now that needs to be said?

When making choices, how do you do it? What is your motivation?

At this point, the particular choices I am referring to were the decisions I had to make in regards to the churches and my family. My priority was staying strong to be there for my mom and Don, honoring myself and honoring my current clients. I was committed to doing whatever it took.

Being there for my family was a no brainer, especially after the love and support they had shown me through the years. Being present for my clients helped me get out of my head and be of service. Being able to give back is the greatest gift.

My motivation was family, service, love, and operating from my heart.

This meant choosing a church. The Ayahuasca church had been my dream. I love working with the medicine and helping people integrate. When that door opened, I thought it was a gift from the heavens.

The exposure to Santo Daime opened my mind to an entirely different approach. I can describe it as being one of God's face-less army of light workers. A team, no hierarchy, only a guardian that oversees and protects the best interest of the church and its members. Everyone was considered equal, everyone had a role, and everyone was welcome.

I thought about how I could do both. That thought faded quickly knowing the split in my energy would not serve either opportunity or myself. I really had to weigh the options and decide. I had to commit to one and honor the path.

I asked myself "what do I want?"

I want to serve. I want to honor the medicine. I want to do what is best for both myself and my clients. I want to do what is in the highest and greatest good for everyone, everywhere, the universe and myself. I went to my intentions. I wanted to travel, to expand, to be led to people, places, opportunities and experiences beyond my current comprehension. I wanted to be part of something bigger than myself, something I may not know how to ask for. I was open to the best path for me.

I surrendered. I asked the medicine, "What path will allow me to honor you, the teachings, and give me the opportunity to be of service? Guide me to the opportunity to be the best version of me and allow you to work through me."

I was open to whatever I received. I went to a 90-minute yoga class, set my intention for clarity, and let go.

The answers were there when I got done. One church would feed my ego, the other my humility and growth. I wanted to grow. I called Spencer, the guardian of the Santo Daime Church and asked about the process. We talked for over an hour as he went through the process in depth. He took his time to make sure I understood exactly what I was asking to be part of. He made sure I was doing this out of my own free will, no pressure and with clear mind. Spencer explained how the ceremony would work and what was necessary. Without going into too much detail, I don't think that it could have happened any easier or more perfectly than it did. Everything fell into place seamlessly and effortlessly. It was magical, to the point of gifts showing up from Brazil, the perfect Elders present, the sun illuminating me like an angel and surrounded with more love than I imagined. There was no question this was the best path for me.

Like all the amazing things that have unfolded in my life, there was more to choosing the Santo Daime path than I could see. I shared that Kirk and Don taught me unconditional love and were the only men that I experienced really having my back. I was scared to lose Don, I already lost Kirk. What I didn't realize at the time was that I was gaining Spencer and Greg. Both had my back. Both showed me the kind of compassion, caring and love that I experienced from Don and Kirk. Neither had anything to gain from me. Both have incredible wives they adore and incredible lives. Both treated me with kindness, welcomed me and helped me because it's who they are. I want to say that again, they acted from a place of love, because that is who is they are.

There have been many shifts and many challenges. Spencer has modeled firmness, courage, strength and integrity. He has helped me really navigate some challenging times with grace and ease. He holds the church and its members in the highest light.

Greg is someone I bonded with instantly. He was and is present with me, without judgment. He is so honest with me, helping me see differently. Where I move through the world emotionally, he moves through the world logically. He was able to help me see the world from a new perspective. Both act in integrity as their actions and words align. It's an honor to have both men in my life.

Reflections

When one door closes, another opens. I was feeling empty and lost as I let go of Gandalf, Henry and others who no longer fit in my life. What I was actually doing was making room for the relationships that did honor who I had become. I made space for men who saw who I was and who I was becoming. I was inviting in men who supported and honored my growth, who valued me as a person, a woman, and a friend. I made space for men who respected me and they were teaching me so much. I love them, just as I did Don and Kirk.

Opportunities

What is your decision-making process?

You've done a lot of writing up to this point, clarifying what you want, who you want to be, where you want to go and what you'd like to feel and experience. What opportunities are being presented to you?

How are you opening up to another way?

Where are you seeing new possibilities, options, ideas?

How willing are you to trust that you are receiving and new paths are unfolding for you? The clearer you are, the easier the path is to see.

What is your willingness to trust allowing you to see?

BITTERSWEET

March

Don's daughter Shelley came to stay with us. She was staying until the end, whenever that was.

We all surrendered to the powers above and were there for as long as it took. The answer came in three weeks. For an intense three weeks I cooked and nourished mom and Shelley so they could focus on just being with Don. There were ups and downs, laughter and tears. I believe everyone was able to say goodbye, make peace, and spend beautiful quality time together before Don crossed. He was able to cross, in our home, surrounded by people who loved him. It was bittersweet.

Everyone needed time to process and heal. Shelley went home to her family, mom needed space to grieve and I needed to find me again.

Six days later, my uncle crossed. My mom and her sister lost their husbands the same week. It got intense. All I could do was be there for my mom. There was no place I would have rather been.

Time. Space. Grieving. Acceptance.
Letting go. Moving forward.

We each had to do it in our own way, following our own process.

Reflections

So many gifts came from this experience. I had spent time with both Kirk and Don, now I was given the gift of getting to know Shelley. She was married with her own family when mom and Don met, I had only spent time with her briefly when they were here on vacations. I was blessed to get to know her light, her love, her kindness, and her. I experienced Shelley as a sister, a friend, a mother, a daughter and just an incredible human. For that I will always be grateful.

I had the honor of being present and talking with a man who taught me so much. I was able to love Don the way he loved me. I was sober and of service to my family. I was able to complete the circle of love.

I have an entirely new relationship with my mom. I no longer robbed her of her energy with worry. I was able to support her and be there in the way she deserved. I was able to love and nourish her. I was able to give instead of take.

Opportunities

We can only control one thing, ourselves. How we (re)act, how we show up, if we are present and able to serve, or distracted somewhere in our heads.

You have a choice, often times many choices. If you choose to face a challenging experience or are faced with one, how can you make the best out of it?

Even in my darkest hours I can look back and see the strength and the blessings the experience gave me. How about you?

Look at one of your greatest challenges, what did you gain?

ALWAYS SUPPORTED

March

The universe was supporting me; my intention of being steward of the land was fulfilled seamlessly as requested. I was given the opportunity to live my dream and move in to a three-story home, on lush property, with many perks. I was surrounded with abundance.

The property was covered in fruit trees, magical trees, peacocks, and so much more. Greg had shown me many of these trees and introduced me to the fruits they produce. I was in heaven. The grounds were private and better than I could have asked for. I found the perfect trees for my hammock. I spent hours with the trees, healing, thinking, dreaming and just being.

The house itself was more amazing than I imagined. There was a closet full of fuzzy blankets, the ones that comforted me as a child, and still do. They are the best to curl up in after ceremonies and reflect. The wall had huge, detailed, exotic paintings. There were priceless artifacts, pictures, and pieces from many different countries. I was astounded at how the universe was delivering.

Spencer asked me if I wanted to go to Hawaii. Ummmm, YES! I was invited to help with a mission that happens there. I wanted to serve and was being given a chance to both serve and travel! Thank you again Universe. I was stoked!

Luckily, I can work with my clients from anywhere. Through all of this transition, I was able to move, travel, maintain my clients, create an amazing Self Love and Self-Acceptance challenge. I was so hopeful that I was finally on the other side of the darkness and the suffering. I was ready to shine.

Not only was I enjoying the new living arrangements, I was really bonding with some of the new people in my life. Greg was quickly becoming one of my favorite people. We would talk for hours after ceremonies and occasionally on the phone. His mind was fascinating to me. He was nothing like anyone I had ever met, and I loved that. He was so unique, kind and fun to talk to. I was learning so much from him and with him. We were on this path of self-discovery together, willing to be vulnerable with each other. He allowed me into his mind and was open to reprogramming. It was amazing the transformations and power he was able to access. He would then offer me so much feedback on everything we were doing. He is very analytical and logical, I am not! He really helped me bridge the gap on communicating with others like him. And by like him, I mean fascinating and brilliant. He's like a computer that processes on a level that is beyond my comprehension. Einstein type processor!

Destiny was like my guardian angel. She has been with the church for a while and welcomed me with open arms and open heart. In the beginning, I unconsciously stepped on her toes. I felt awful and didn't know what to do. I was scared. I called her to let her know what I had done. The anxiety inside me was so intense, but she needed to hear it from me. I was prepared for the worst and she showed me the best. Destiney was clearly not happy to hear my news; and this exposed her true self. She responded with kindness, love and acceptance. Her core was pure light. At first, I didn't believe it. I carried fear that somehow there was more and it would come back to haunt me.

It never did. Instead, she had me over for dinner. She offered me resources and made sure that I was prepared for our trip to Hawaii. She continued to show me kindness, support and help me. Destiny showed me many things, most of all that she had my back and was a true sister, friend, and source of pure love and light. On top of all that, she sings beautifully. Her voice heals. She channels hymns, teaching and sharing through her words, her music. She harnesses the energy and lights the way for others with compassion and grace. I learned so much from her, especially how she handled overstep. She taught me by how she treated me and shared some secrets on navigating other minefields. I have so much appreciation for her.

Stephanie is another angel. She is an actress, play write, and genuinely kind human being. She is also Spencer's wife. She is gifted on many levels. To witness her during the works is awesome. She's magical to watch sing, as she always sings with a smile. Even when she is struggling, she snaps out of it in seconds and is so present and firm. She's incredible. Stephanie goes out of her way to say hello, acknowledge and welcome new people to the church. She cares deeply and shows it as she interacts with the attention, curiosity and passion of a child. Her presence is so innocent, engaged and special. She also sings these magical little hymns that make everyone smile and fills them with joy. My favorite is about Minh's dog! She sings to the dog and the dog dances with her. We see the world very differently. Stephanie appreciates how I see the world, the depth, the faces in the flowers, spirits in the trees and the magic that many don't even notice. I love spending time with her and learning how she sees the world. Her kindness, generosity, acceptance and love radiate.

The universe was preparing me, strengthening me and showing me that I had the support necessary to move through another illusion. I had no idea I was about to be shattered again. It felt like sucker punch. A woman, Maria, whom I loved and trusted, allowed me to see her shadow. She was the reflection of the life I thought I wanted. She helped me see the possible outcomes in what I was asking for on so many levels. I was able to witness what money, control, and leadership can bring out in a person. I witnessed the path I was heading down. It was clear to me why I chose the Santo Daime Church. It was clear to me where I was out of alignment. It was clear to me that what I believed I wanted and what I really wanted were two different things.

Maria was someone I sought spiritual advice from on occasion. When we first met, she emanated love. I was drawn to her immediately. She was beautiful, happily married, well-traveled, had a couple homes, and seemed to have it all. I frequented some of her healing circles and really enjoyed talking with her. I thought we bonded and I trusted her. She had my back on a couple occasions when I was really struggling and being pushed to be stronger. She could tell that I needed compassion and healing at that point. She talked to the circle about knowing when to push and when to practice self-love and have compassion. Compassion for self and others. I really believed that we were friends, allies, sisters. I shared some secrets with her and started spending time with her outside the circle.

The closer I got to Maria, the more I started to see. I was invited to spend time with her and another member of the circle, Ken. I was excited. She shared her ideas and plans for what she was building. It was all in alignment with what I wanted. We all seemed to be co-creating something. Ken and I were spending time together working out the details. There was some definite friction between he and I, however I thought we all had each other's backs and best interest at heart. I could not have been more wrong.

It was within a couple of weeks of Don's death when it all came crashing down. I was set to meet with Ken and Maria to talk details about a project. I also needed to meet with a client prior to, so I got permission from Maria to work with my client at her home before we met. Her home was huge and on a giant lot with tons of privacy. I went early. No one was there yet, so I chose to sit outside on one of the decks to work. About half way through my session, Ken showed up and entered the space. I shared with him I was working with a client and would appreciate privacy to honor my client. He agreed and stayed. So I went inside. He came inside. I didn't understand. I went back outside and was able to apologize to my client and finish the session.

Ken never left the area. There was five acres and multiple floors and decks to Maria's home and he insisted on being in the same space. I was furious. I was more reactive than I should have been, I know this, I was grieving. I started crying and was really angry at Ken. We were arguing about why he would not just respect my session and go to a different area while I finished as Maria walked up. She heard us and wanted to talk with both of us.

We sat down and I owned my anger. Snot was running down my face, I was crying and I was letting go of so much pain I had been carrying. Pain I didn't even realize was there. I owned it I took full responsibility for my actions and that I knew I was overreacting. I was shocked at the response. When Maria asked what happened, Ken shared how horribly rude and out of line I was. He explained all my anger was completely for no reason and that I was just out of control. Maria agreed and added, 'Yes Willow, I could hear you walking up. You sound so angry."

I was so confused. I was angry. Don just died. I was grieving, just moved and was really moving through some intense pain. I had just admitted all that. I again apologized for my behavior.

I agreed. I owned it. I needed compassion and understanding. Instead I got shamed. Maria explained that I reminded her of herself and many other fiery women and she no longer thought she could trust me. I was in awe. This spiritual leader who schooled the circle on light, love, compassion and acceptance didn't care how much pain I was in. She didn't acknowledge my loss, my apology, or taking responsibility for my overreaction. They both sat there and told me what a jerk I was. It was a nightmare. I sat there in silence and cried harder as they continued to tell me what was wrong with me.

I was so grateful for the contrast and the clarity. It was amazing to be able to see clearly before going to Hawaii and be able to make decisions about what was next when I returned. What I discovered was another opportunity from the universe to guide me. Greg had sent me a video that helped him, it was about NLP (Neuro-Linguistic Programming). I can't explain what happened, but it unlocked something. I was discussing options with another friend from the church and sharing my thoughts. We were both brainstorming about our next moves. The conversation led to him introducing me to a good friend who teaches NLP.

I love how the path, the best path, really does unfold easily and effortlessly when you're in the flow. The next certification course was scheduled about a week after I was returning from Hawaii. It lined up magically. I signed up, confident that this was the next logical step. It felt amazing. Everything just felt right. There was no question I was asking for everything I needed and the universe was delivering seamlessly as requested.

Reflections

Maria was another gift. She was a reflection of the path I was originally asking for. She headed the circle and was the gate-keeper, the gatekeeper I would have been had I chosen the other path. I was able to see that without team and accountability; the power really can get the best of you. I was able to witness how out of alignment she was. This is something I could only see because it was me. The contrast to who she projected and who she was allowed me to see myself. I was able to see that the power I was seeking was false. The experience assured me I chose the right path. I was able to surrender, grab the golden nuggets of wisdom and let go of everything else quickly.

Opportunities

In my experience, I was seeking a feeling and believed the experience would give me that feeling. I started seeking the feeling rather than the experience I believed would create it. So much shifted.

Look at a time you got exactly what you wanted and it was nothing like you expected.

It could be a relationship, event, experience. Something that you really wanted and believed that it would be perfect. What did you believe it would be like?

What is different than you expected?

What did you learn about yourself?

What clarity are you gaining?

EVOLVING

Imagine one of your best friends, someone you confide in, share your secrets with, trust, and laugh with. Think of all the good times. Now imagine going through one of the biggest transformations of your life and calling that person. You are in pain, needing to talk and expecting support, the support or conversations you were used to. Instead, what you get is shut down. Imagine calling a friend with a challenge neither of you have ever experienced and being told what you should do. How would it feel to share your heart and be met with the words "just get over it!"? Or "you have to do it this way." And be cut off every time you speak.

This was a woman we will call Jill and her experience with her friend Izzy.

Jill got sober and had been on a personal growth journey. Izzy supported her upgrades, choices and growth. They had an incredible relationship, both being very artistic and creative. They fed off each other's creative energy. Most of the time they spent together was creating. They talked about personal stuff, however as Jill grew, she confided in Izzy less and less. She was experiencing her friend being very judgmental, closed, and critical of her decisions. Izzy often had very strong opinions of how others 'should' handle things. Especially things she had no experience with. Izzy had not gone through many of the things Jill had, and it became painful to share with her. So she really focused on the creative parts of their friendship. Throughout the years, Izzy went through experiences similar to Jill's and asked her for advice, apologizing for her earlier judgmental attitude.

The friendship seemed to be evolving when it took a turn. Jill appreciated the presence and friendship that she and Izzy shared, but was really thinking that even the creative part wasn't working anymore. The more she lowered her tolerance, the less time she and Izzy spent together. She realized that every idea she shared, Izzy ran with. Izzy created it and shared it as her own before Jill even had a chance. Jill even loaned her some tools and Izzy went crazy, making all kinds of stuff. The creativity was great! However, at the time, Jill was really moving through a painful growth spurt. The two grew apart. Izzy made incredible gifts and creations for their entire network with Jill's tools. She really is talented. She showed them to Jill, so excited about everything she was doing.

At one point she even said," Thank you Jill, look at this beautiful gift I made with your tools. You need this. "

Jill felt bad about their distance and the feelings she had for Izzy. She felt guilty for thinking Izzy was insensitive and disrespectful of their friendship.

And then Margo walked up. Izzy took the gift away from Jill and said, "this is for Margo. I was just showing you since I made all this stuff with your tools."

Jill explained that all she could do was stand there, crushed as Margo snatched the gift, held it to her heart and just stared at her.

Later, in private, Margo inquired why she and Izzy don't spend time together anymore. She proceeded to share how awesome Izzy was and all the fun things they were creating and how much fun they had together.

Jill called me wanting to process. She was still moving though something and needed support.

She felt replaced, dismissed, and like her friends didn't care about her at all. She had made some other choices from a place of pain that caused her even more grief. She felt like she was spiraling out of control and needed help making sense of what was happening.

Jill came to some pretty powerful discoveries. She realized that her growth was disconnecting her from people, places and experiences that no longer served her. Just like getting sober and upgrading herself, this was another upgrade. She reflected on the relationship and came to the conclusion that she was the one that was different. She used to be Izzy, that's why they got along so well. She realized that she used to take everyone's ideas and run with them as well. She couldn't wait to show everyone what she made. She also realized that she was doing it to feel liked, worthy, important. She was able to see Izzy differently after seeing the reflection of her own past behavior. She was even able to see that Margo was very similar to who Jill used to be. It all made sense. Izzy was still the same Izzy. Jill was just not the same Jill.

It opened up the dialogue for us to really dive deep into Jill, why she was drawn to the friendship and why it was no longer working. The self-discovery was painful and freeing. Jill chose to explore different circles and ways to bring out the best of herself. She found people who allowed her to show up, enjoyed her and helped her cultivate her crafts. Izzy didn't seem to notice that Jill drifted away and that told her everything she needed to know. She accepted that they are on different paths and was so happy with her new circles she no longer felt the pain and loss.

There were many layers to this that we uncovered. It took me back to something I learned from Susun. Don't rob people of their joy and purpose. For example:

Don was unable to do as many tasks now, however the tasks he could do brought him joy. His got the mail, took out the trash and recycle, and emptied the dishwasher. These were all things my mom could have done faster, easier, and without thinking. The thing is, they gave Don purpose. They allowed him to serve, participate and show up. My mom recognized this and wanted him to feel as much life as possible. She would walk by the mail box as it was being delivered and NOT grab it, but instead, let Don know it had been delivered and ask if he wanted to get it. His face would light up, he He had purpose, he was alive and he would walk out eagerly to get the mail. To many it would seem like nothing, however my mom realized to Don it meant everything.

At the end of the day, what Jill realized was that sometimes you just outgrow people. She had been doing so much internal growing, and when you change, not everyone is going to like your upgrades. We all evolve at different rates, and that's ok. She was able to release herself from Izzy with love.

Jill laughed when she told me about her experience with another friend, Mary. After working through the Izzy thing, she could see how she created her own pain. Mary was the daughter of a powerful mentor and leader that Jill looked at like a mother. She would turn to the mother occasionally for advice as she was learning to value herself. She wanted to be closer to both Mary and her mother and she was reflecting how she tried too hard. Mary often shared stories of people she loved and experiences she really valued. Jill wanted to be one of those stories. She wanted Mary's love and support.

Jill offered Mary a service in exchange for feedback. Jill realized, as she was sharing with me, how unfair this was to both her and Mary. She was offering a service to someone who didn't ask for it, with an expectation. When she didn't get the feedback, she felt hurt and rejected. She took it personally.

After really talking it all through, Jill came to the conclusion that she was never after feedback, she was after the love, support and friendship she already had. She was attempting to prove herself or create a self-worth that was not necessary. Mary adored her, and her feedback was irrelevant. How can she possibly give constructive feedback on a service she didn't want or need?

Jill learned a powerful lesson. In the end, Jill realized that Mary was a blessing. The experience was a gift for Jill to value herself, her time and herself. She shared her breakthrough with Mary. The two women are able to laugh about it now. She was so happy.

Reflections

I used to brag about a high tolerance, until I learned that it actually equals low standards. People who love themselves don't treat themselves, or allow others to treat them, poorly. They set the example by treating themselves with respect, honoring their time, and valuing their services.

People, places and behaviors we once accepted leave our lives quickly as our standards change. It's ok. Let them go with love, knowing that the space will be filled with those who have standards that align with your own.

Practice discernment. Be careful who you share your ideas with. The person you choose can feed your inspiration, crush your dreams, or steal them. Protect yourself, your ideas are your reality. Surround yourself with people who see possibilities.

Don't give away your gifts and services with expectations. Either give freely, or only give when asked. When asked, get paid. Value your craft. You set your standards, your value, by how you value yourself.

Value yourself. Value your work. Value your time.
Value your energy. Be the example.

Opportunities

Where in your life are you holding resentments?

Who have you given to with expectations?

Really reflect on the experience and ask yourself what you were seeking?

Now, how can you reframe the experience to empower and take responsibility for yourself?

CONTROL

There was so much to learn from Max and Erma. From the outside looking in, the challenge was obvious. I had lived it and seen it many times with many couples. Control. They were each trying to force the other into their box. Neither wanted to understand the others view. Each believed their perspective and way of doing it was the best and only option. Filling a void, the perfect match and mirror. They were perfect for each other, until they weren't.

When they first met, Max had the power. Erma looked up to him, saw him as someone to learn from. Erma surrendered and was eager, willing and excited to learn. They spent so much time together, had fun and it was great, until Erma grew. Erma started stepping into her own power, learning, making decisions that Max didn't like. When the balance of power started to shift, the love affair turned ugly. It went form a perfect match that was more like mentor/student, father/daughter, guru/student to a power struggle. In reality, neither were fully in their power. Each fit the others need. When the need of the student was fulfilled, the teacher loses purpose, control and no longer feels safe in the relationship.

They then became perfect mirrors, fighting for control. Each complained of the other's behavior.

"If he would just... Can't he see..."

"If she would... Can't she see..."

Perfect Mirrors. Neither could see that they were exact mirrors, each trying to change the other to fit their needs. Both thinking they knew what was best for the other. He would tell her how to parent, though he's childless. She would tell him how to surrender, though she hadn't. Each schooling the other on what they really needed to help themselves. And when they got along, they turned it on me and told me how I needed to change to fit their needs. They loved to tell me what was wrong with me and how I 'should' do everything! Both desperate to control everything and everyone to fit into their perspective. I could see the cycle.

This is something that I had to work through in my own life. It was painful to recognize the reasons we attract the same person each time. And we will, until we choose to love and accept ourselves fully. When, and only when we love ourselves, will we attract another who loves themselves. This is when love becomes love and the relationship is healthy.

Two people are attracted to each other for exactly who they are, not their potential. It took me a while to really get this. It wasn't until I fell in love with me and accepted all of me that it made sense. If there is something about your partner you want to change, look in the mirror.

Max and Erma took some time apart to really look at themselves. They both chose to do some inner work and answer some hard questions. They are still together and choosing to accept the other as they are and look at themselves. They hear, seek to understand and support each other now in a very different way. They learned and continue to learn about themselves and each other. It's beautiful.

Reflections

We really do attract the perfect match. Victims attract an abuser/bully, both gain from the exchange. The victim feeds off fear and manipulation. The abuser provides validation, approval, attention, the story the victim needs to embrace the role. The abuser gets attention, uses power, feeds ego.

You have the power to choose to stay or leave. Many people choose to stay, feeling stuck.

Stuck is refusing to see options, possibilities. Stuck is allowing things to stay the same and refusing to take responsibility. You have the power to change. You have the power to make new choices. There are tons of options if you are open to new possibilities.

Focus on what you want and new opportunities will present themselves, but you have to be open to see. You have to be willing to take responsibility, recognize your situation is a result of your previous choices, then make new choices.

Remember, if someone is trying to control or change you, it's a reflection of them. They are teaching you what they need. If it triggers you, look at yourself. If it doesn't, you have the choice to listen or not. You can kindly say, "Thank you for sharing your opinion" and walk away.

Opportunities

Look at your relationships. Reflect on the patterns. What are you seeing?

What is the reoccurring theme for you?

Where can you take responsibility and make new choices?

What are your new choices?

Write them down. Own them. Feel them. Empower your new way of being.

ADDICTION

It was painful to encounter the twenty something version of myself. She was beautiful, sweet and captivated the attention of many. She lived with a man and had many others on strings. They described her as love. They were easily seduced by her charm, her voice, her affection.

She attempted to get close to me. I was skeptical at first, but opened up to see. It had been so long since I played that game, I almost didn't recognize it. The art of seduction, manipulation, and false love, what I believed at the time were acts of love. I now understand to be acts of desperation.

Desperation. It was the addictive behavior. It took me a long time to fully understand the depth of the dis-ease. Just because we stop using our substance of choice, doesn't me we are free. I have seen people that have not used for years and are still very sick. The substance of choice is a band aid. Until the mindset is changed, the only thing changed is the form of bondage.

The mind of an addict tricks itself. They believe that if they are not using the original substance, alcohol for example, they are healed. In reality, many actually just replace the substance with something else; work, exercise, love, service, etc. Some replacements aid in the recovery, others are just as toxic. To truly recover, one must change their thought process.

This woman had been sober from alcohol for a few years; however, she was still very sick. She knew it and I knew it. To those who are who are not addicts and don't understand the game, she creates an illusion of sweet and loving as she slowly and methodically lures them in. She masters finding their weakness and pulling them in deeper. Before they know it, they are stuck and have no idea what happened. Her seduction and manipulation are so subtle, sweet and gentle. To all outsiders, she has created the illusion of the perfect victim, innocent and sweet.

She was a master at stories and creating ways for others to rescue and help her. Her prey never saw her coming. She would complain about the man she lived with, her lover, to bond and get the attention of others. She would then seduce the prey in a number of ways to bring them closer. If the prey had a lover, she would tell the lover stories to hurt her and drive a wedge between the two. She would position herself to the other woman in a way that was hurtful, creating the illusion that her lover already betrayed her. Her goal, make his lover question him and go away. The seductress would then sweep in to comfort him and tell him how much he deserves better, as she lured him in closer.

The men are clueless, they can't understand why their lover is upset. All they see is what the seductress wants them to see. They never see the behind the scenes manipulation to drive the wedge between the women they care about, and that actually care about them. They have no idea how their life falling apart is actually a strategic plan orchestrated by someone wanting their undivided affection.

It's a sick game. I invited her to stop. I offered her some options. She declined. Instead, she looked me in the eye while purposefully manipulating a mutual friend. She drove a wedge between him and his girlfriend, between us, and created chaos. She positioned herself in a way to look vulnerable. She wasn't ready to quit and consciously chose to raise the stakes.

I hugged her and thanked her. I thanked her for showing me what kind of sister, friend and woman she was and told her how much I appreciated her. I did. I learned so much being on the other side. I was also able to kindly cut ties with her.

Luckily, the truth always comes out and the couple was able to find their way back to each other. The man realized what he had and returned before it was too late. His lover was mature and cared about him enough to forgive his wandering and work through the experience. This isn't usually the case. Many times, this behavior ends badly for everyone involved; it's toxic.

I reflected on when I was that deep in my dis-ease and that desperate. I was able to accept her without judgment, knowing that when I acted that way, it came from fear. Fear and self-hatred. No woman that loves and respects herself would act like that. In my experience from working with many women and being there myself, it's the most extreme form of neediness; having no self-worth, and no clue how to actually connect to another human being.

Reflections

Even after being sober for a few years and having grown in so many areas, love was the hardest to understand. I used to use promiscuity to get attention. I thought it somehow made me attractive. I gave myself away believing it would make you love me. It was desperation and survival. I thought I had to prove myself and wanted to be chosen. I didn't think I could take care of myself. I didn't believe in myself. I was afraid, alone and ashamed. I lived it for most of my life and can spot it anywhere. I had to choose not to enable her, but to release her and move on. I did this for me. I loved that version of my past, accepted it and gained so much from that experience.

She had a choice and she chose to stay. I respected her choice.

It's beautiful to no longer be in the competition to be chosen, but in my power and able to choose. When you love yourself, you can accept everyone for who they are without judgment.

You can also choose whether you want to spend time with them or not. You have a choice.

Opportunity

When you are vulnerable and needy, you are a target.

Where are your vulnerabilities? What emotions are you seeking to be filled?

How can you fill that need yourself?

How can you prepare yourself for challenges?

Who do you trust?

BE SKEPTICAL AND OPEN

When Jeff first contacted me, he had been hiding like a hermit for over a year. He was experiencing heart problems and admitted to me he thought he would be dead by summer. It was already March, which didn't give him much time, he had to act NOW! He was trapped in a story that the doctors gave him and focused on what he believed to be inevitable, death. Jeff was overwhelmed with fear, fear of unfinished business, and regrets.

In just three months, Jeff's entire life changed. He transformed his fears into excitement to live. Jeff no longer needed heart surgery, and his medical appointments were reduced rapidly. His body healed itself. His energy and desire to live, love, and laugh increased exponentially.

Not only did Jeff's health improve at a rapid rate, so did his lifestyle. He went from hiding like a hermit to becoming an active member of his community. He now enjoys parties, lunches, and many other encounters with the people who love him. Jeff has reconnected to a life that promotes living.

As Jeff's energy and vibrancy returned to him, so did his business. Jeff's new found zest for life, willingness to tell a different story, openness, all restored his creativity. He is an artist and this creative energy coupled with this new life force opened up many opportunities for him to shine. His business is booming again. He generated many new pieces and attracted more clients. It's beautiful.

In three months, Jeff went from a perceived death sentence to fully living life again. His desire to change his perception led him to explore mindful thought changes while continuing medical observation. He transformed his entire life. A road trip he once feared has already become a reality. He bought a camper, packed up his dog Oscar, and went out on the open road. He sends me pictures of breathtaking views. More than anything, he is enjoying living.

Reflections

Jeff is a powerful example of rewriting your reality. He did it. He made the choice to live. He chose to call me. He made the choice to invest in himself. He was willing to see the world differently, get out of his comfort zone, change his story and make new choices to support that story. His decision changed his entire trajectory.

Opportunities

Look at an area in your life where you may feel like you are out of options, powerless.

How long will you allow yourself to suffer before opening up to new possibilities, choices, and perspectives?

Where can you get a second opinion? Third? As many as it takes?

How bad do you want something better?

THANK YOU UNIVERSE

May

When I got back from Hawaii, I needed some time. I needed silence. I had not stopped in over a year and needed to ground, reflect, be alone. The dream home was beautiful, however no longer felt right. I learned so much living there and was appreciative of the people, the experience and the opportunity, however it was time to move on. There was a lot of action, energy, and movement. I needed the opposite. I needed solitude. I again surrendered and asked the universe for a safe place to just be for a while.

I let go and planned for my NLP training course. It was a week away. After that I was scheduled to watch my mom's pets for a week or so while she went to Michigan. She wanted to go spend time with my brother, his family, and wanted to see her sister.

Another request delivered seamlessly and effortlessly. Mom wanted to go to Michigan for longer, maybe a couple weeks. She asked me if I'd be willing to stay longer and take care of the animals. I agreed and told her to take whatever time she needed.

I knew how important visiting my brother and spending time with her sister was to her. They both had some healing to do.

She sent me a copy of her travel plans; she was going to be gone for a month. Tears of gratitude ran down my face.

I spent about another week in my dream house before packing up. I had six weeks planned out and I trusted the next step would appear just like all the rest. I had my NLP Coaching Course and then a month to just be. A safe place to unpack all the stuff I had been carrying.

I packed up what little I had, said thank you and left. I wasn't sure if I was more excited to learn NLP or for the month alone. I had been going strong for almost 14 months without stopping to process and integrate. It felt like I was on the personal growth and self-discovery fast track. I was exhausted.

Reflection

For me this was clarity. I knew exactly what I needed, silence. I asked and then I surrendered and trusted. It showed up as perfectly as it always does. The more I trust and surrender, the better life gets.

When I moved to my dream property, I thought it was going to be the silence, the healing, the opportunity to reflect. It was the opposite. I can see all the red flags were there and I chose to ignore them. I wanted it to be something different. I can see how it was me stepping out of my flow and thinking I knew best! I was focused on the illusion and not my gut. Once there, everything about living on that property felt forced, uncomfortable, challenging. It looked like I wanted, however, it felt horrible.

I lied to myself and learned a powerful lesson. If it's not easy, trust the resistance and wait. Luckily, I learn fast. I was able to quickly let go, surrender and bounce back. It was a powerful experience to step back out of the illusion. I had to be willing to be wrong, trust and redirect. It was a beautiful opportunity for growth on many levels. I was able to transition with grace and ease, effortlessly. Once I let go, I was back in the flow.

When I trusted the universe, what I received was better than I could have asked for. I can feel the difference when I want something and force it. Humility and surrender are the quickest ways back into the flow. I didn't care what anyone thought, I was willing to be wrong and move on without any more resistance.

Opportunity

Think of a time you wanted something and forced it. Did you keep pushing against the red flags, resistance, and challenges?

What happened when you finally stopped pushing, forcing, fighting the resistance?

Where can you apply surrendering to current situations?

What are you forcing that you are willing to surrender?

Write out what you desire and just let it go. Trust that the universe will answer your request better than you could plan! Be open, allow.

NLP AND THE POWER OF WORDS

May

Jason Schneider and Perception Academy delivered. I took a deep dive, 80 hours over 8 days. Like everything I asked for, it was exactly the perfect stop before taking the time to unpack. I learned so much about words, programing and reprograming. More importantly I learned more about myself.

NLP stands for Neuro-linguistic programing or simply put, learning the programming of your own mind. Not only do you learn the programing, you learn to reprogram. This to me was another language just like everything else I had been studying. It's a new way to understand how one see's the world and associates meaning to anything. It's a simple way to reframe that meaning in order to support one's highest potential.

During the course of the week, my neediness was revealed to me. It enabled me to sit back and observe myself, witness my own behavior, and see my perfect reflection; the need to be seen, heard, and validated. I saw how I was excited to have the answer and show how smart I was. I saw how I often wanted to share another view and a personal story. I felt myself want to speak and then stopped. I watched this behavior in others. I listened to their stories. I made a conscious decision to observe in silence, especially when I wanted to speak.

We did a lot of partner work and practicing on each other. Everyone experienced life altering breakthroughs. The experiences I had repeatedly were perfect for me. I had a partner who was my perfect mirror. Someone who was so excited to be right and have the answer, be the hero. Instead of listening to me and asking questions, helping me pull out my own truth, my partner would jump in with their interpretation of my experience. The help they thought they were providing me actually just made me cry. I looked at myself and wondered how often I had done this to others. It was something I had been conscious of and working on since I first lived with Susun four years prior. I know I had made huge strides and I felt like I was under a microscope releasing the last bits of that energy. The only way to truly empower someone is to allow them to discover their own truth. The best teachers and coaches don't give the answers; they empower through questions. The more this person interrupted and tried to lead me, the more lost, angry and confused I got. His intentions to help me and tell me what he saw only pushed me deeper into the hole I was crawling out of. I saw an older version of myself clear as day. That impact was branded on me. I felt the power of what I was learning. The impact of receiving what someone else believed to be help was painful. Lesson received, downloaded and imprinted permanently. I needed it to end. And end it did. Jason modeled how to set myself free. It was priceless.

I learned about anchoring emotions. In NLP there is no need for the stories, only the emotions. We learn how to elicit the emotions we want and anchor those emotions. Once anchored, it's easy to access them quickly and easily. It IS possible to cancel out emotions we no longer find useful and replace them with desired feelings. It's amazing what power we have and how we can use it. It can be done using all five senses, along with many other options.

Jesse kept popping into my head and this all explained why. I unconsciously anchored love to him. Wow! What a breakthrough! During his first Ask Me Anything, when he kept asking "What do you want?", I wanted love. My desire was so intense. I had been asking to align with love for so long. I had asked for blue eyes and so much more that he represented. The feelings I tapped into every time he asked were powerful. His eyes were magnetic. Staring into them evoked feelings so intense that his eyes and voice became anchors. After that, every time I saw him, I was flooded with love. NLP is all about evoking emotions and setting anchors. The purpose is to free people; however, like everything, it can be used in many ways. It was all making sense to me, I just needed to reprogram myself!

It was interesting to observe the emotions that I went through during this process. I realized I projected so much onto this man. I was embarrassed. I felt stupid. I looked at the video I sent him, the videos I put in Legacy, and felt like a complete idiot. I went through shame, guilt, fear, and a range of other emotions. I had obsessed over him, believing with every cell in my body he was the man of my dreams. I was almost too embarrassed to ask Jason for help, but I did. I asked him to remove the anchor and reprogram me. He did. We replaced the anchor, releasing me from the obsession and allowing me to keep the feelings I felt in a healthy way.

Reflections

Jason and NLP really helped me understand how to ask even better questions. It's funny, because I thought I had been asking better questions! The cool thing is; there is always room to improve. Jason was good at redirecting and not getting sucked in by people's stories. He was fun to watch and to work with. I learned so much from him about how to really create and enforce healthy boundaries with compassion, kindness and concern. He was an excellent teacher.

Opportunities

What would it be like to see yourself?

Step back and witness or observe yourself, what do you see?

Separate yourself from the story and just feel; what do you feel?

When you look at the people in your life, is there a common theme?

What can you learn from that theme?

Is there anything you would like to change or shift?

What's stopping you?

TIME TO UNPACK

May

I was finally alone. I wasn't sure where to start. It had been over a year since I was alone, really alone and able to sit in silence. Silence for an extended period of time. I meditated daily, but this was different. I was able to relax in a way I didn't even realize I had been missing. I was decompressing.

Decompressing after so much stimulation was uncomfortable. I knew I had a time limit and started pressuring myself. My mind went to the things I should be doing like focusing on my business, figuring out what next, etc. I started getting triggered and began emotional eating. I instantly recognized the pattern, I was stuffing my emotions with food, or avoiding them. I was not going down this road again. I chose to fast instead. I gave myself permission to just be for three days. I told myself I was stronger than my emotions and set out to prove it to myself. I knew it only took three days to reset the system and clear out sugar and other toxins, so I did a three-day water fast.

The experience opened up more questions than answers. I felt like I was losing my mind. I felt like I had to show up for other people. I felt like I needed to dive in immediately and work on my business. I looked at what I was doing. I felt like I had to be doing something. Everything I tried failed. I was forcing it. I had to get back into a state of surrender. I didn't know how to stop. I was feeling conflicted. I didn't realize that I was actually carrying a backpack that had filled up over the past year. The process happened so slowly that I didn't even feel the added weight until now. And now, I didn't know how to put it down. Somewhere along my journey I regressed from surrender to survival and it scared me. I was on system overload and malfunctioning!

I screamed and asked for help. "Thank you, now help me PLEASE!!!"

A question my mom had asked me flashed through my head;

'Isn't there someone who can do for you what you do for others?' referring to the energy sessions I do.

She had experienced it, read my testimonials, and I had done sessions at her house. She heard the transformations and witnessed them. Lis was the only person I had experienced the same relief with when I was in NY.

Mom had asked several times over the years and I always blew it off; I worked through stuff daily through yoga, meditation and some other ritual work. I was usually able to get through it on my own. Not this time, this was huge. I knew I could do it, however, I wanted help. Her words were in my head; I was open to receive help. I was learning to receive, period. This was an opportunity to ask for help and I was ready.

I had no idea with who, or how I was going to release. I thought about doing it myself or calling Lis. I asked the universe for guidance.

I was guided to Chris Bale. I heard his voice, watched his videos and read the testimonials. I needed to release the energy. I needed to release the pain from my body, from my cells. I requested a session. Chris was booked until after my mom returned. This wasn't going to work for me. I was willing to commit while I knew I was alone. After mom returned, I wasn't sure where I would be or if I would have the space to surrender to the session. I know from my own work that if I cannot fully let go, then there is no point. I had to be the client I want, willing to show up with 100% trust and willingness. I gave him my timeline and explained that I only had a short window. I thanked the universe for guiding me to him and asked that if this is what will help me, then please make it happen. I let it go.

I reached out for more help. I opened up to Nicole and Cher. With their support and encouragement, I went within. I was creating a new 21-day challenge for my women's group. I did a guided meditation for them and took them inside to discover what would help them most. Each woman decided what the challenge would be for them. I did the same. I needed time and space to process. I challenged them to take an hour a day to focus on what came up for them. I invited them to make this challenge very personal. I committed to sharing what I learned and set out on a personal journey of my own.

I heard from Chris, he had a cancellation and was able to meet with me the day I was breaking my fast. Thank you, Universe! I then went deep. I committed to a 5 day fast. No technology, no food, no noise. I needed to let go. My body and nervous system were in dire need of a reboot. I needed guidance. I needed to stop "needing" and figure out how to get back to surrender and peace. I honestly had no idea how. I chose to practice what I preach and just be. I had been here before. The only way to find the peace and clarity I longed for was to stop searching. It takes time. I had not realized how hard I had been going. I was not aware of how much the constant stimulation affected me and how difficult unpacking it all was going to be.

The quieter I got, the more I learned. What I discovered answered everything. I had been reliving high school since I got sober. I have been unconsciously recreating the events and attracting versions of the people I gave my power to back then. I had been systematically taking my power back and upgrading both myself and my experiences. Wow. Wow. Wow.

I reflected on many relationships. When I was 15, I had a huge crush on a boy in my class I will call Nick. He asked me out. I was ending a one-year relationship with someone else that was leaving for college. I cared about them both, but was drawn to one more. One was going to college and one I saw every day. My heart was torn; however I made a choice. I said goodbye to the one leaving and explained why. He understood and asked for one last kiss. I agreed. Nick happened to drive by at that exact moment. He was angry. He thought I lied to him. I tried to explain, but he wouldn't listen. My entire senior year, I blamed myself and tried to earn Nick's trust, love and attention back. We would drink, he would make out with me, tell me how much he liked me and then the next day tell me what a whore and a slut I was. I kept going back, somehow believing I deserved this abuse. Believing I betrayed him somehow and owed it to him to fix it. Every man I have dated since has been a version of Nick. I was attracting abusive men, believing I somehow deserved it. This was not conscious. I was so stuck in the victim mode. I was stuck in prove myself mode. That year is when I started drinking, escaping, hating myself and having suicidal thoughts. I had been stuck in that cycle ever since. I even married a man who put me in the hospital. I was in so deep I had no idea. It was so clear to me now.

When an addict starts using, they stop maturing. I was emotionally stuck at 15 for the majority of my life. I had moved through and upgraded in many areas, however love paralyzed me. I kept choosing the wrong man, until I stopped dating all together. Then when I would try again, I would pick the one man that didn't see me or excepted me to prove myself. I would push away the men who did see me, respect me, and value me to seek the attention of the one I needed to be worthy of and prove myself too. It was a cycle I had been reliving. I wanted love so bad and was so scared at the same time. I was scared because I obviously had a very delusional idea of what love actually was.

My attraction to Jesse represented another cycle, only with a new outcome. I started out wanting to earn his love, prove myself, get his attention. I didn't even realize I was doing it at first. Jesse didn't engage. In the past, the men had been working through their own issues, and fed my desire to prove myself. Not this time. Jesse actually talked of this in Legacy and spoke of the cycles and roles we play. Susun worked with me on this too. I got it; I just didn't realize how deeply imbedded this pattern was. I really had to reflect on what I was discovering about myself. I was having a breakthrough and needed to go deeper.

I thought Jesse was the man of my dreams, but did I really? When I had the opportunity to meet him, I didn't. I resisted the urge. Somewhere inside me I knew it wasn't about him. I knew it and now it was all making even more sense. Jesse happened to be the one man that didn't acknowledge my craziness. He allowed me to have my experience without engaging, or even knowing what was actually happening to me.

I had to look at my own behavior, my obsession. I asked myself, why didn't I want to meet him? At first, I thought I was a paralyzed fifteen-year-old girl with a crush. When I saw him, I had no idea what I was experiencing. It wasn't until Lori helped me understand those feelings! Feelings I had never worked through before. But there was more than just having a crush. I was bold, I was fearless, I chased and went after what I wanted. I already made an ass out of myself to him, this wasn't it. I wasn't paralyzed by my crush or fear of rejection. In my mind, he already rejected me. What was it? Why did I choose not to talk to him?

My intuition. Yes, I was guided not to. Why? I needed to know what I was really experiencing. What am I uncovering about myself? And then it hit me. Intentions. I set very clear intentions to only act in the highest good of everyone, everywhere, the universe and myself, with harm to none. That's it! Thank you Willow! I set up a safety to stop myself if I was acting in a way that was impure, not in my highest potential. At that time, I was obsessed with Jesse in a very unhealthy way. I was so attracted to him and really believed he was the man of my dreams. I was obsessed with the projection I created of him, not the man standing in front of me. I wanted his attention. Who? The man in front of me or the story I created? This is exactly why I was guided to walk away. I needed to discover my own truth. It was an opportunity for me to feel that energy. I became fully aware of its presence. And for the first time, I resisted the urge or temptation to give in to it. Holy crap! What a powerful realization.

I was so grateful I never said a word to him. I was so grateful I trusted myself. I am so grateful he never acknowledged me or gave me the time of day. I was so proud of my ability to resist temptation, trust, surrender, listen, look within, and recognize my pattern.

It was painful. It was beautiful. It was the clarity I was looking for. I cried. I was so grateful for what I was discovering. The universe was delivering everything I asked for brilliantly. And with every breakthrough, I needed a release. I realized how much pain I caused myself. Pain I was needlessly carrying. This cycle had lasted twenty-eight years. The thought made me sick. I was ready to let it go.

Ready and willing, it was time to meet with Chris before breaking my fast. The session was exactly what I needed. Chris held space with so much love and compassion. I cried, I screamed, I released so much pain that I had stuffed. I released years of trauma from the cellular level and was refilled with love. He showed me how it felt to have a man show you love when you're hurting.

The experience gave me a new model of what loving support feels like. Out with the old and in with the new! The best part, he did it all from Spain through Zoom. I was safe and secure in my own space.

I was weak for a couple more days. I nourished and loved myself as my body recalibrated. I embraced the silence. I journaled. I listened. I normalized my new way of being. The calmness was so strange at first. I didn't know it existed. I had never experienced this feeling. I thought I was there already. There was an anxiety inside me that had been there so long.

I had not noticed it; until it stopped. If you have ever been in a room when the quiet hum of an appliance stops and it's silent, this is what I'm talking about. The second it stops, that melting, the calmness, the serenity you didn't even realize you craved completely washes through you. I don't know how long I laid there in silence, all I know is that if Yoda (the dog) had not needed to go out, it would have been longer. I didn't want to move.

I no longer had any needs. I didn't care about anything. I had nothing to prove, nothing to hide. I appreciated everything so much and for the first time really was just in a state of peace and bliss beyond anything I had experienced before. My drive was gone. I didn't care about my business. I had no fear of missing out or being left behind. I almost felt numb, but it wasn't like before. This time it was a healthy numb. It's hard to describe, maybe like cloud 9, only better. I felt whole for the first time.

And then the flow set in. The inspiration hit. I was writing and channeling like crazy. Again, exactly what I asked for. That is when I started this book.

Reflections

All the answers are within. You must be willing to turn the projection to introspection. Silence, meditation, and reflection are our greatest tools.

I have a deep love and appreciation for Jesse, the work he does, the space he holds and the fact that he didn't acknowledge me. I appreciate that he trusts himself and shows strength by not feeding the need. He didn't belittle it either. He left me with it, to self-reflect. It's a priceless gift, to allow one to have their own experience. My experience freed me.

Opportunities

I'm going to ask you again to look at your relationships. The patterns you wrote down previously. What is the root of that pattern?

Who did you feel powerless around that you can reclaim your power from?

Get silent. Take the time to go deep. You are worth it. Challenge yourself to look deeper. You have the power to free yourself.

MORE ANSWERS

As I wrote, I had many more breakthroughs. I had asked for love, laughter, and joy. I asked to fall in love. I did. I fell in love with myself. My journey took me through every version of myself, giving me the opportunity to accept, love and integrate those versions; to see my experiences through my new eyes, new awareness and new perspectives. It allowed me to fully understand how much all that pain I went through taught me. I learned how valuable EVERY experience was. I saw how important each person is. Everyone played their role perfectly.

My journey started with George, the neediest most un-present version of me. The part of me I pretended didn't exist. The version who would overcompensate to prove my worth or how smart I was. The desire to be needed was exhausting. He was a reflection of that desperation to be seen, heard and validated. I was able to transform that energy into willingness, humility and self-care. I learned to seek my approval and follow my standards without compromise. I forgave, then fell in love with this version of me. Once I did, once I accepted and loved myself, I was able to move on without blame, shame, guilt or fear. I stopped taking on other's people's stuff and trying to fix it for them. My only responsibility was me and the more I tried to show how special, smart or valuable I was, the more I pushed people away.

Susun taught me to honor myself, stand in my power and use my voice. She taught me to trust myself. To be aware when something is out of place, someone is acting funny, or the details don't add up. I did. I love her so much for all I learned from her; she has been one of my greatest teachers.

Alice was a reflection of where I came from, so trapped by fear she was afraid to see the truth. That was me in my addiction. I used to be afraid to answer the phone when I owned a gym. I was afraid of conflict or the person on the other end being upset with me. It made no sense. I was so scared of living, I numbed myself and hid. I indulged in other people's pain and problems to feel alive, important, or just feel anything. The anger, rage, and victim mentality fed me. It was my source of energy. I had no idea how to be happy. I replaced that energy with hope, willingness, surrender. I chose to look at myself and take responsibility for my actions and my situations. Once I owned it, I had the power to change it.

Henry showed me where I was vulnerable, gullible, and lying to myself. Deep down, I knew I was not special to him. He was very clear about his motives to win. He taught me how he hustles, and made it clear he doesn't commit. He knew what I wanted; I was clear. He knew how to seduce me and pull me in; I taught him. Each time I left him, he worked harder to get me to come back. He got better at his game and I got better and seeing the illusion. I let him in believing it would be different and figured out the new game quicker. I wanted love so desperately, I compromised me, my boundaries, my worth. I transformed all that energy into loving me, honoring me, and figuring out what was important to me. I learned to ask better questions, enforce my boundaries, release the need and walk away. I found I would rather be alone than with someone that doesn't respect me. I now spot a Henry a mile away. I love myself so much for understanding the illusion and how I was drawn in. I love myself for being strong enough to walk away.

With Gandalf, I saw how he chose to take the perceived easy way out. I remember being fearful and thinking I need this job. I saw that version of me that was handed the opportunity I had been asking for, to be the light, and then choose fear. I saw how many times I could have made better choices, but didn't trust myself. I could see when I chose to compromise my integrity, my work, myself; out of fear. I once chose to stay with the people who encouraged me to surrender myself over honoring myself. I now choose to surround myself with people who have my best interest at heart, not just how they gain by my attachment, neediness and fear. I was able to walk away from him with love, forgiving myself. I was able to turn that energy into power, confidence, trust, and confirmation. There was no question I made the right choice when I walked away, both times.

Lis was an incredible teacher. She connected me to stepping into the power Susun unleashed, only with love, compassion and grace. I saw the version of me I was becoming, channeling the power differently. I needed Susun when I was stuck in my rage and anger. I needed Lis to show me how to do it with kindness. Lis was the version of me that stopped fighting and learned to control my emotions. To harness the energy and use it for good. To teach with kindness, humility and laughter. I fuel that energy, charge it and focus it on possibilities.

The seductress allowed me to see that version of me and how it felt being on the other side. I remember when I played those games, it was out of fear and low self-worth. I lied to myself at the time, scared of what I might see. Looking back, I can see how scared and desperate I really was. It was a beautiful reflection and test to see how much I had grown. She is a beautiful woman, making her own choices, choices I once made. I chose to not play or enable her game. Instead I loved her and left her with herself. I harness that energy now vs waste it. I honor my boundaries and plug those energy leaks. You cannot help someone that doesn't want to be helped.

I look back at the yogi, I reflected on our friendship. It ended because we made a deal. After the deal was made, she changed it out of fear. I remember the call. We were creating an event and agreed on a price. She changed it without discussing it with me. When I asked why, she said she asked her pendulum. I remember feeling that powerless, afraid to talk it out, and giving my power to an object. I remember how passive/aggressive she was with men. I remembered when I used to accept behavior from someone and then try to change them. I remembered thinking if I...then they will... It never worked. It was never about the other person; it was about me loving myself enough not to compromise my self-worth.

Cher was a beautiful mirror of self-expression. She is an amazing artist that didn't paint for years. Someone destroyed her work and she stopped creating. She then started again and her work, her expression, is magical. She reminds me of me, I wrote as a teen and then someone read my journals. The violation was so traumatic I stopped writing. When I stopped writing I got stuck. We were both finding our voices again. We inspired each other and supported each other's growth.

Nicole is a rock star business strategist. She is the version of me I outsource! She is logical, numerical, analytical, totally my opposite. However, she is great at bouncing back and forth between clouds and grounding. She is extremely curious and attentive. Nicole seeks to understand, asks a lot of questions and is extremely humble. She is fabulous at stepping out of emotion and seeing the bigger picture. She uses her logic and creativity to help businesses, and especially artists, shine. She is another example of women lifting women and seeing the best in everyone.

Minh is like a brother to me. We come in and out of each other's lives. We started our journey together when I was an addict. We have moved through so many experiences together, always having one another's back. We may not always see eye to eye, however there is no question of intent. We learn from each other, hold each other accountable and pull the other up. He is part of my soul family and we will always answer the others call. It's like the bat signal! I love him and always will.

Destiny was and still is an angel, she helped me move through my aversion to the light. Originally, I was skeptical. Her kindness and acceptance were so pure and genuine. I learned so much form her and how she navigates situations. Her presence, support and lead allowed me to step into that light and normalize the new me.

Greg saw me, my gifts. He appreciated me, and I him. He was so open and present. He has many gifts, including his mind. He is a creator. He showed me the power of reprogramming. I watched him upgrade himself and observe himself. He's a genius.

Spencer is definitely a reflection of where I am going. He helps me rise by modeling firmness. My experience with him reminds me of Don, a man completely in his power. He has an incredible wife he loves dearly; they are a beautiful couple. They are generous, kind, understanding and magical. Witnessing Spencer go through some really hard times was a priceless gift. When others were throwing stones, he stood in his integrity. He did not engage in the war of words, finger pointing and proving. He stood firmly in his commitment, his word and his integrity with honor. It wasn't easy; however, he rose above and came out on top. I'm proud to have him as a guide.

Stephanie is kindness, generosity and love. She models inclusion, acceptance and is so genuine. She learns about people with the curiosity and attention of a child, that priceless excitement and attention many lose as adults. She's a true angel, sister and friend.

Mike is a true lighthouse. He leads by example, putting people over profit. He has been behind many magic curtains and exposes the truth. He reminds people to keep it simple. Mike leads by example with love, integrity, compassion, kindness and grace. He was kind to me when I was hurting the most. He's honest, authentic, and real. He loves his family and people in general. Mike constantly reminds people that it's not easy, however it is worth it. Keep your head high. Mistakes are part of growth. Highest energy wins, focus on what you want.

Mike is the reflection and model I stepped into. I learned so much from his unwavering authenticity and heart.

Jesse. His presence illuminated where I was vulnerable. The experience exposed where I once fell prey. I went from attachment, hope, and desire all the way to complete aversion, anger and disgust. I was able to see every version of me in my reaction to him. This experience taught me so much about myself, swinging from one extreme to the other, then back to myself. The journey released me from my need, allowing me to navigate with clarity. The power of observation and witnessing exposed many layers for me, layers I am grateful to have a better understanding of. I appreciate the role Jesse played in my personal evolution.

Reflection

I can say that looking back through all the versions of myself changes perspective. Nothing is separate, everything is a reflection. I was able to really appreciate every experience to the fullest, knowing I created it. I was able to fall in love with me, accept all I have been through and integrate what I learned. I am different, one choice at a time, constantly rewriting my reality to support my upgrades.

I replaced older models of behavior with new ones. I put all that I learned into place and created a new version of me, one that completely loves and accepts me, ALL of me.

Opportunities

Make 2 lists of all the people in your life that have impacted you.

One list of experiences you didn't enjoy and one of the most amazing people you've met.

Next to each person, write out what you think about them.

Now, look at what you wrote. How is that you?

What is that teaching you about yourself?

For the not so nice experiences, what did you learn?

What did the experience teach you to watch out for and pre-pare for?

For the amazing people, amazing experiences and people you appreciate...turn the appreciation around. Love everything about that person in you.

They are all reflections of you, who you have been or where you are going. Learn from the pain and focus on where you are going.

You have a choice, who do you want to be?

LOVE

I set out on a journey to experience love, and I did. Like everything, I did not find it where I expected. I released myself of attachments, learned how to truly need nothing and appreciate everything. I learned so much about what love actually is, and isn't.

Love is so overused in our culture as we love everything from cookies, to mommy to sex and rock and roll. To really understand love, I needed to define what love means to me. This is what I decided.

Unconditional Love doesn't exist, as unconditional is a condition. A condition that confuses and misleads people to believe they have to accept or tolerate behavior that doesn't feel good. I no longer think of love as a destination or having anything to do with another person. It has to do with one thing, me and how I feel. To me it's acceptance, understanding, valuing both myself and others. It's knowing that I am always safe, secure, protected and connected to all that is. I say all that is because God, Source, Universe and other terms create limits in the mind. All that is, includes all that is. It's like being in the forest. I can choose to stay in the forest, see the forest and feel the forest as long as I like. I need no one to have this experience with me. Others can join, they can come and go and it doesn't affect me. I hang out and I can leave. I can wander far away and experience the desert if I choose. It's all up to me and what I choose to feel, tap into, experience.

I was open to the myths and alternative thoughts about love:

- M: You complete me.
- A: No one can complete you; you are a complete.
- M: Confusion around the source of Love.
- A: It doesn't come from an external source; you are the love. It's within you and you have unlimited access to an unlimited supply.
- M: You can lose love:
- A: You can't lose a frequency
- M: I want/need that person
- A: I am attracted to or desire connection with the essence of that person

Healthy Love is me wanting for you what you want for you. Me taking responsibility for my feelings and allowing you to be responsible for yours.

I am no longer afraid of 'losing love'. I cannot lose what is inside me.

Fear of losing love creates neediness. Like attracts like.

Other powerful tidbits:

- Feeling trapped is a result of refusing to focus on possibilities.
- The conditions of your life are the momentum of previous choices.
- There is no right or wrong way, only what's right for you, right now.
- Focus on what you want, the feeling, the essence.
- Trust that you are getting what you asked for.

- A glow stick needs to be broken to shine, trust the process.
- There are 2 sides to every experience. We need both. If you have never been trapped in the darkness or experienced pain, how can you possibly appreciate and value the light?
- We can only comprehend equal and opposite, meaning we can only experience bliss to the same extreme we felt pain, there has to be a reference point. The contrast is what makes the highs so high. Appreciate the experience that showed you that joy.

Each person, each role, each experience has value. The addict is equally as valuable to society as the president. Through all these roles the dualities allow us to feel and experience each so that we can make better choices.

Examples: condemn   < >   forgive

Judgement   < >   Open Minded

Blame   < >   Take responsibility

Indifference   < >   Caring

Control   < >   Surrender

Resist   < >   Accept

Excitement   < >   Boredom

Project   < >   Reflect

I learned to be flexible, open, detached and to observe; to respond vs react. To follow what I feel, not what I see. It's a dance and I finally understand my rhythm. I trust my flow. I know I can navigate any storm and stay in the sea of love. I'd love for you to join me.

Reflection

Getting clarity on what love is to me helped me see differently. Taking responsibility for myself and allowing others to have their own experience freed me. Letting go of seeking and tapping into myself allowed me to shine.

Opportunities

How do you define love?

How do you take responsibility for your own experience?

Make a list of ways you can love yourself.

Describe what you want to feel. Then close your eyes and feel it. What does your forest feel like?

GIFTS

These 14 months were a roller coaster, the ride was exciting, painful, fun, enlightening and magical. I experienced so much contrast. Reflecting on how my intentions played out, perfectly engineered to maximize my expansion, is beautiful. I am impressed. Not just with the magnitude of the delivery, but also with the fact that I handled it so well. I went from spiraling out of control to being in perfect stillness.

I learned so much on the journey. I saw so many versions of myself. I couldn't have done it if I wasn't willing to look at myself, take responsibility for my life and get out of my comfort zone. In order to make new choices, I had to see what else was out there.

You don't know what you don't know, until you know!

The trick for me is finding the equilibrium. Many people seek balance, but to me balance keeps you stuck. To be perfectly balanced is to be paralyzed, you can't move or the balance is off. It's more about finding the ebb and flow, working within parameters you need to stay in alignment with your core self. The clearer you can be on what you want to experience, the easier this is. You flow in a direction, adapting to the unknown.

Life is like a river, there is a current and a natural flow. Surrender to the current and it will carry you. Fight the current and it will exhaust you. Get out and be still, witness, observe; you never know what you are going to see. There are so many options. The only question that matters is what do you need right now. What do you want to experience right now? Then what is the best next step to achieve that goal?

Get clarity, feel yourself experiencing exactly what you want to feel. That was the biggest challenge for me. It took me a while to figure out to stop seeking things; money, clients, love, etc. and tap into the frequency. How do you tap into a feeling or frequency you've never had? How do you tap into love when you have never felt it and don't understand the feeling? This was my challenge. I had to build a model. I did this through contrast and getting out of my comfort zone.

I had to have experiences to find clarity. Does this feel good? Is there anything that doesn't feel right? What is this feeling?

I met several people that I learned from. I would learn and make better choices next time. The trick was not getting caught up in the emotion of an experience I didn't enjoy, but rather understanding how I created it and learning how to make better choices. It's all about choices, the next experience is only one choice away.

There were so many individuals that really helped me understand what I wanted and what I didn't. I was able to see the contrast between people in power who empower others vs people who consciously attempt to disempower others.

Having witnessed these models and many more allowed me make better choices. The more I experienced and witnessed, the more I had to choose from. This is why it is so important to get outside of your comfort zone and outside of your routine.

It is equally important to then take the time to process each experience and integrate what you learned. I feel like I went on the fast track. I remember saying I am willing to experience more pain to go faster and get to the other side. Looking back, I'm not sure I would say that again. I have been going nonstop for over a year. To then sit, decompress and unpack; it was hard.

Carrying that much was heavy. It was so heavy, and so full it made it more difficult to decipher at times. I can see where the load clouded my judgment and had I taken the time to reflect sooner, I may have saved myself some pain. I also know, I had to have that experience to know that!

I wouldn't change a thing. Each person, each experience was a gift. I expanded and upgraded myself on so many levels.

Reflections

Every experience is a gift. Release yourself from the emotion and learn. Embrace the journey, it's always teaching you something. The more present you are able to be; the better choices you are able to make. You've got this!

Opportunities

What can you do today to get outside of your comfort zone?

How can you change your routine? Do it backwards!

What are the gifts you receive from each person you choose to spend time with?

What are your most valuable golden nuggets gained through pain?

What contrast are you creating to bring clarity into your life?

What are the people closest to you modeling?

How do these behaviors empower you?

HOME

I am finally home, in a sea of love. My heart is open. I have the core people in my life. My relationships are healthy. I have experienced so much love, laughter, community and joy.

The more I surrender, trust and allow, the more the universe reveals to me. I am in a total state of surrender and flow, appreciating everything and needing nothing.

I had to let go of everything to gain more than I could imagine.

It took a while for my mind to comprehend it. Can it really be that easy?

Ask. Feel. Surrender. Trust. Silence. Inspiration.
Action. Experience. Do again.

The process of redirecting, rewriting my life was intense, and worth it! When rewriting your reality, the important thing to understand is that it doesn't happen overnight. Think about the shift like a plane going in for landing; it's a series of subtle shifts. If the plane attempts to dive to quickly, it would potentially crash. It has to flow with the changing winds, the changing pressure, potential storms, and the birds. There are no shortcuts and the pilots have to adapt to whatever may spring up, all while caring for the safety of the passengers. When you want change, it's one choice at a time, creating the new reality. Put in the course, surrender to the flow, and you will eventually arrive at the destination. The trick to a smooth flight is adaptability and flexibility. There will be storms, there will be winds, there will be challenges. The more you can enjoy the journey, the easier it will become. Before you know it, you are so happy, life is so amazing, and you are there. It's no longer about a destination, but about appreciations and how much you enjoy the reality you are creating. You really can have it all.

Let go of everything you thought you knew to gain more than you ever imagined.

PEER REVIEW

Peer Review is the process that came out of this amazing journey. It's how I work through my own challenges and what I share with others.

Here's what is stands for and how I integrate it into my life.

Each experience is just that. When triggered, that is when it truly is our greatest opportunity for personal growth. We have the option to react or seek enlightenment. I used to think enlightenment was a destination, something for the select few, gurus, and spiritual leaders. I now believe that enlightenment is the process of lightening the load, releasing what no longer serves me. As I let go of false beliefs, attachments, strict rules and limited perspectives, I am lighter. As I practice more understanding, acceptance, love and compassion; I am lighter.

In my experience, the more I am unwilling to see another perspective or the more I seek enlightenment, the more lost I become. It is within. It is the process of seeing ourselves in each other. You are a reflection of me and I of you. We see what we perceive from where we are. When we accept one another without judgement, love ourselves and our brothers and sisters; that is enlightenment. When we expand our perception and recognize that we are all love at the core, that is enlightenment. Nothing happens to us or for us, but rather is an interpretation and projection from within us. We see what we look for. Contrast teaches us and allows us to be human and experience the full spectrum of emotions, experiences, and choose different behaviors.

So you have a choice to see the world, others, experiences however you wish. It's free will. When not understood or operated from a place of fear and lack, it creates pain and suffering. When we operate from love, understanding and compassion; that is enlightenment.

When I get trapped in my emotion, that is when I experience pain and suffering. When I am able to elevate my view, my perspective to see all sides, that is when I feel the love, joy and freedom I set out to find.

I trained myself to see the view of my peers, as we are all equal. I call it the **PEER REVIEW**:

Pause – Pause, Breathe

Elevate – Rise above the emotions, emotional reactions and limited view reactions

Expand – Broaden the perception, open awareness to include multiple perceptions, seek understanding

Remember – What is the intention? What is the desired outcome and how can it be reached with a win/win/win scenario? How can this be resolved with love, compassion, and acceptance

Respond – Clarity, Compassion, Love and deliberate action or deliberate inaction, not everything requires to be dealt with immediately. Time and space may be the best response. No response is a response. Take as long as needed until there is clarity. Ask for guidance if needed.

Empowered – When ready to respond, is the response from an empowered place for all parties? There are ways to respond from an empowered stance that doesn't disempower others.

Value – Value yourself and the others, as humans as individuals with respect. To value another doesn't mean you have to agree, it means you can respectfully disagree. How can this be valuable? New insights, new perspectives, new understandings?

Integrity – Act in integrity, be sure that the words and actions are in alignment.

Explore – Look at self and see what else is possible? What else can be learned, acknowledge, gained from this experience.

Wisdom – Savor the golden nuggets and enjoy your more enlightened, wiser self. Take in what you learned and apply it to your future. Journal, take notes and really reflect to see how this information can be integrated for future choices.

You are invited to use and apply this concept to your own life. For support, community and to learn more visit www.GroovyWillowGreen.com.

EPILOGUE

I have learned so much along this journey. Publishing this book took twice as long as I anticipated. Why? Because I rewrote it several times. I rewrote my reality as I wrote this book.

I was forced to slow down.

I chose to look at exactly what I was creating.

The part of me that was controlled by time, space, and need was released. I had to trust the process; trust that I was being guided to what I asked for. I had to release all control of how it showed up and what it looked like. If I had known what to look for, I would already have it! I had to trust what didn't make sense and be open to what showed up. I have learned that the more I try to control what it should look like, the longer it takes to get what I am asking for. When I surrender and follow my gut, I am led to exactly what I didn't know I needed.

Fred and Ginger, not their real names of course, are a couple that flew in to work with me during this process. Ginger had experienced me before, having had a massive breakthrough and shift. She wanted her lover to experience the same kind of breakthrough. Fred had some not so pleasant luck and was open to another way. Her goal was for them to evolve together. She saw this as an opportunity for him to release old patterns and upgrade his energy and for both their energies to stay aligned with each other.

When they arrived, we began the work the first evening. Ginger had a tremendous experience. Fred resisted. The next morning, Fred dug his heels in even deeper. He refused to show up for what he asked for. He was unwilling to have the rest of the experience. I released control and handed it to him, having zero interest in wasting my energy. I opened the experience and gave him 100% control over the plans, decisions, events and experiences. He took us on an incredible journey. It was fun and I learned some things.

When I asked questions, he chose to be elusive and did not communicate what we were doing or how to best prepare for the experience. I soon learned his motivation was finding the best drinking spots. He wanted alcohol, asking if I minded if he had a drink or two. I did not mind; it was his experience. He did have two, then four, then more and added several shots of liquor to the mix. As he drank his personality quickly escalated into a very different version of himself; one that was opposite of how he showed up.

The next morning, I offered another opportunity to experience what he came for. He declined, offering many excuses. He said he felt transformed and was enjoying his experience.

He wanted me to provide the same experience for his friends. He made clear they were seeking XYZ and that was how I needed to show up if I wanted to work with them.

What this story highlights is how much the need to control actually blocks us from the very thing we seek. Fred had a great time because it was all about Fred. There was no co-creation or allowing me or Ginger to show up and be a part of the decision making. Ginger went out of her way to create this experience for Fred, to expand him and assist him through his challenges. Instead of being open, he resisted. He has no idea what he missed out on. He couldn't surrender and let go of control. It was painful to witness someone fighting for their limitations. It was equally enlightening as I reflected and wondered where I can surrender more control. What am I missing by being unwilling to let go and allow someone else to take the lead? How can I lean into the experience, release more control and be open to the possibilities?

What I learned was that the past will continue to test me and present itself. I will always have opportunities to recreate the same experience with different faces. I will also have equal opportunities to be open to something new. It takes strength, confidence and trust to face adversity to stand for something new. The unknown can be scary, but equally as exciting if we choose to be open. We see what we expect. I expect joy, learning, adventure and expansion.

I have a new set of intentions.

I see and draw to me, through divine love, those Beings who seek enlightenment through my process.

I enjoy mutually beneficial expansive experiences on a scale greater than my mind can comprehend in this moment.

I love how easily and effortlessly everything is always working out for me; unfolding divinely in ways that are more joyous, loving and magical than I could have planned.

I appreciate having all that I need, before I know I need it; with plenty to spare, plenty to use, plenty to share and plenty to save.

I surrender, trust, and allow myself to receive; knowing that I am guided, guarded and protected at all times.

I joyfully embrace my upgrades integrating easily and effortlessly.

A personal dream is to meet Ellen DeGeneres and be on her show.

Dear Ellen,

You are to me as Dian Fossey is to you. She dedicated her life to enhancing the lives of gorillas, you have dedicated yours to humanity.

Through all the adversity and challenge you have faced, you show up and promote kindness. Your ability to turn your pain into humor that uplifts others is priceless.

You have so much power and use your voice to give, to spread joy and give others a voice.

Thank you for shining your light and illuminating so many people, opening up possibilities that some can only dream of.

I know I'm not alone when I say, "I am inspired by your generosity. You are a gift, leading by example. You have made me laugh and brought joy into my life though some of my darkest days and I appreciate you."

I would love to meet you and hug you, so I am writing that opportunity into my reality.

With Love,
Willow

I set these intentions for the highest good of everyone, everywhere, the universe and myself, with harm to none. So Be It And So It Is.

I chose to trust what didn't make sense, surrender to possibilities I could not see and trust my intuition and instinct. It felt like I was losing everything. It hurt, it was confusing and I wanted to give up at times. I'm so glad I didn't give up. I am so grateful I trusted the process. I had to be willing to lose it all to gain more than I could have asked for. All I really lost was suffering, attachment, judgement, and desire to control. The path led me to more joy, expansion and understanding than I could have comprehended when I started. It's amazing how easy and hard it is at the same time. I can say, it's totally worth it!!!! Life gets better every day. My relationships get better every day. I am pleasantly surprised as the more I surrender and let go, the more I actually gain. It's liberating and freeing. I love life today in a way I never imaged possible. If what I am saying is resonating with you, and you are ready to let go of everything to gain even more, I invite you to take the same leap of faith.

PEER REVIEW is only possible if you are open to seeing the world differently. Would you like to let go of your programming and unlock the ability to see multiple perspectives, multiple views and unlimited possibilities?

What do you look like from third person?

What do you look like to an ant?

What do you look like from the view of an eagle?

How would you receive yourself from another angle?

This is only the tip of the iceberg. When you start to explore these views, these perceptions open your mind to unlimited possibilities.

A great way to really tap into the abyss of infinite wisdom is through creative flow. Opening the mind to other views and perspectives allows you to get outside of yourself. You open up to make believe and magic. This is the space where the impossible becomes possible. The possible becomes probable and from probable your mind can allow it in. From probable your mind can start creating a map to bring it into your reality. And just like that, you are rewriting your reality, turning what was once impossible into your new normal. Your mind starts only seeing possibilities.

So the only question is where do you want to start?

What possibilities would you like to write in?

What do you want to experience?

What do you want to feel?

What else is there?

How much more love can I feel?

How much better can it get?

How much more can I receive?

Who can I draw in that will expand my capacity for joy, abundance, co-creation, community, health and wealth on a scale beyond my wildest dreams?

What amazing minds want to co-create an experience with me that is mutually beneficial and expansive for all who choose to show up?

Who wants to unleash the creative flow and see just how abundant, fun, and unique it really can get?

Who wants to work with me to unlock worlds, experiences and opportunities that blow our current level of comprehension out of the water?

Who is ready to expand their mind?

These are the questions I am asking. If these questions resonate with you, you are the one I am calling in. I invite you to learn more at www.groovywillowgreen.com.

ABOUT THE AUTHOR

Photo Credit: Johnny Wechs

Life has been an interesting journey from codependency, addiction, and self-hatred to the ultimate freedom, Self-Love and Radical Self-Acceptance!

I was misunderstood, angry and never felt like I belonged. Doctors, psychiatrists, and specialists gave me all kinds of labels and pharmaceuticals to mask my pain. I self-medicated with many other things, spiraling out of control until the day I chose to ask a new question; Who am I without all the labels and addictions?

I went through a transformational experience of unbecoming who I was told I was and discovering my own truth. Remembering my authentic self. One choice at a time.

Each choice is a path. A path lighting the way to the next choice. The more I was willing to see and let go of, the lighter I got. It's amazing how easy it really is, yet how hard at the same time. Enlightenment is a journey of self-discovery. It requires vulnerability, honesty, and it gets ugly. I had to be ugly to be free. And now all I see is love, beauty and the magic in every experience.

To honor my path is to stand in my truth, authentically. To see everyone in their highest light, living their highest potential.

Having unlocked a world of unlimited possibility and new opportunities with every choice, there is nothing I love more than helping others do the same.

My passion is working with others, helping them connect to their own power, possibility and passion. It's so rewarding watching others experience personal freedom, joy and an improved quality of life!

My educational background includes an Occupational Science degree with focus on personal training, Certified Shamanic training through The Foundation for Shamanic Studies as well as a Shamanic, Herbalism Apprenticeship and Internship with Susun Weed. I owned a fitness club for 4 years. As a personal trainer, my specialty has been working with Parkinson's Disease, post-stroke, and rehab clients for over 10 years. I learned the power of the mind and how it can influence Dis-Ease based on the "thoughts" and "attitude" of the client. That led me to becoming certified in NLP (Neurolinguistics Programming) and really going deeper into the power of positively reprogramming one's mind.

My application of a very unique and diverse set of credentials led to tremendous success with clients both one-on-one and in small groups. My ability to connect with clients, right where they are, and guide them to find their own truth is a gift; a gift I embrace, as it transpired from my personal journey through the fiery depths of darkness.

HOW DO YOU CHOOSE TO SEE THE WORLD?

Imagine a world where you see everyone in their highest light, with love, compassion and

Imagine a world where you see others in their highest light with love, compassion and acceptance. Everything and everyone is a mirror and can only be judged if judging. To see triggers as opportunities to gain a deeper understanding of self. Understanding that will set you free from your own shadows, blocks, misconceptions and false belief systems. To be open to new understandings, perspectives and beliefs. To be open, yet skeptical and choose wisely. How would it feel to fully trust your feelings above all else, trusting your intuition?

Imagine how the world would look knowing that each person has their own truth built from their own experiences, understanding and upbringing. How would it feel to trust that everyone is doing and acting the best they can with the views they have and the tools they possess? You can be the light that's sets them free!

Imagine the peace to no longer believe in right and wrong or good and evil. To instead seek understanding and open yourself to another's view. Everything is relative depending on whose view you are looking from. Imagine seeking to explore how many other views there actually are and understand them. The more perspectives you are open to see, the more compassion, wisdom and knowledge you gain. It's a journey of awareness.

Everything is a choice.

I see magic, light, and love because I choose to.

I choose to see the best version of you as that is actually a reflection of me.

What do you see?

What would you like to see?

Words are spells.
That is why they call it spelling.

White Magic: Using the word to empower, uplift, educate, create, illuminate the highest light, highest potential, source view

Black Magic: Using the word to hurt, gossip, hate, spread rumors, or paint a picture that is unkind and unnecessary

I invite you to see everyone as a sister, a brother, mother, father, son, daughter, friend, human. We are all one, moving along our path, evolving at our own pace. The more kindness and compassion we show each other, the more we all gain. Together we rise.

More Reflection Opportunities

What do you want?

To go deeper?

You can download the workbook with bonus content at www.groovywillowgreen.com.

Visit www.groovywillowgreen.com to learn about opportunities, workshops and check out the current schedule of events!

CPSIA information can be obtained
at www.ICGtesting.com
Printed in the USA
LVHW091359141120
671373LV00005B/333